T0347725

ABOUT THE AUTHORS

Theodore Trefon is a senior researcher at the Belgian Royal Museum for Central Africa and a lecturer in environmental governance at ERAIFT/Kinshasa. His previous books include *Congo's Environmental Paradox* (Zed, 2016) and *Congo Masquerade* (Zed, 2011).

Noël Kabuyaya is an assistant professor of human geography at the University of Kinshasa. This is his first book.

GOMA

Stories of Strength and Sorrow from Eastern Congo

Theodore Trefon
and Noël Kabuyaya

ZED

Goma: Stories of Strength and Sorrow from Eastern Congo
was first published in English in 2018 by Zed Books Ltd,
The Foundry, 17 Oval Way, London SE11 5RR, UK.

Originally published in French under the title
Précarité et bien-être à Goma (RDC) in 2016 by L'Harmattan,
5–7 rue de l'École Polytechnique, 75005 Paris, France.

www.zedbooks.net

Typeset in Book Antiqua by seagulls.net
Cover design by Emma J. Hardy
Cover photo © Robin Hammond/Panos

A catalogue record for this book is available from the British Library

ISBN 978-1-78699-141-6 hb
ISBN 978-1-78699-140-9 pb
ISBN 978-1-78699-142-3 pdf
ISBN 978-1-78699-143-0 epub
ISBN 978-1-78699-144-7 mobi

CONTENTS

PREFACE AND
ACKNOWLEDGMENTS

The wherewithal to carry out research for this book was provided by the GeoRisCA project, which was funded by the Belgian Federal Scientific Agency (Belspo) and coordinated by my anchor institution – the Royal Museum for Central Africa (MRAC) in Tervuren. GeoRisCA contributed to risk management strategies in the Great Lakes region of Africa by assessing and analysing natural risks (volcanic eruption, earthquakes, landslides and erosion) as well as socio-political problems related to the region's legacy of insecurity and violence, vulnerability and unpredictable governance dynamics.

My involvement in the design phase of GeoRisCA was instigated by Caroline Michellier and François Kervyn, who recognised the pertinence of probing people's perceptions of risk before attempting to modify attitudes and behaviours about urban planning, civil alert and civil defence strategies and emergency management. Interdisciplinary in its design, this set of personal narratives helps put the natural science and policy findings of GeoRisCA into sociological perspective. This book builds upon previous research experience and can be considered as a sequel to my two other urban sociologies: one about Kinshasa (2004), the other about Lubumbashi (2006).

Goma: Stories of Strength and Sorrow from Eastern Congo is the culmination of a stimulating collaboration with my friend and colleague Noël Kabuyaya of the Human Geography Department at the University of Kinshasa. Noël and I have worked together on various projects over the years, so, when it became clear that GeoRisCA would be able to recruit a Congolese researcher, I did not hesitate in asking him to partner with me. Co-authoring these narratives remotely from two continents was not stress-free but our relationship of trust enabled us to bring the project to fruition. Noël, who speaks French, Swahili and Kinande, spent ten months in Goma from April 2013 to January 2014, first to get to know the cityscape and its inhabitants and then to carry out the in-depth interviews upon which these stories are based. I visited Goma six times between September 2012 and October 2015, also to familiarise myself with the city, decide which social universes to explore, and work with Noël on finding the right research balance between vulnerability and resilience. My subsequent visits to Kinshasa enabled us to work together on writing once Noël returned there from Goma.

We drafted a three-part research questionnaire with sections focusing on the identity and background of the people interviewed, the social, economic and administrative aspects of their work, and themes ranging from basic needs to existential preoccupations. Key examples of these latter topics include physical security, social and professional rivalries, the Nyiragongo volcano, access to food, water and energy, family relations, housing, recreation, belief in religion and witchcraft, money, sickness and death, healthcare, well-being and perceptions of the future.

Once Noël started accumulating information, we devoted a lot of time to Skype discussions on how best to decode and transcribe the meaning of people's accounts; then we initiated a long phase of structuring and processing the information before starting to write it up section by section. Neither of us worked on this book project full-time, so the writing phase took over two years. When the stories were in nearly final draft form, Noël and I spent three months together in Tervuren in front of a computer screen finalising the manuscript – which was in French.

Catherine Dom read and commented on an early draft of the manuscript and made useful suggestions for improvements to both style and content. Armèle Jonniaux copyedited the revised draft, which was then shared with Pierre Englebert, Philippe Jacob, Bogumil Jewsiewicki and Patrick Welby, who also made insightful recommendations, particularly on my introduction. Charlotte Gérard did the final copyedit and the manuscript was then handed over to the MRAC publication service, supervised by Isabelle Gérard – after further comments from two anonymous reviewers were addressed. *Précarité et bien-être à Goma (RDC): Récits de vie dans une ville de tous les dangers* was published in 2016.

As the production phase of the French-language version was drawing to a close, I contacted Ken Barlow at Zed

Books to inquire about a possible publication in English. After Zed accepted our proposal, I started the rewriting and translation process, which took six months. This gave me the opportunity to correct some of the imperfections in the French version by eliminating information that did not seem necessary for readers in English and by adding contextual facts and background. Direct quotations were of course translated as closely as possible to respect the voice and style of the interviewees. Judith Forshaw meticulously copyedited the manuscript, taking particular care to flag whatever hints of French idiom remained in the translated version.

Many individuals helped us in Goma, providing information, facilitation, guidance and friendship. Bernard, Élise, Emery, Éric, Gédéon, John, Lucas and Onésphore are some of them – and are identified by their first names only for reasons of political sensitivity. Noël and I were present in Goma during some difficult moments (during the M23 rebel occupation, for example) but we never felt threatened or in danger because these friends made sure we did not take any unnecessary risks. Nearly seven years have gone by from when I first had the idea to write this book to its publication in English. Sally Coxe and my children Lea and Basil caught glimpses of me sitting with my laptop, sometimes mumbling to myself while translating and editing: I hope seeing this volume will satisfy their curiosity. Amy Shifflette provided inspiration throughout the research, writing and translating phases by expressing enthusiasm and by extending level-headed advice. While all of these people are warmly thanked, our greatest debt is to the protagonists of these stories and the other wonderful people of Goma. We respectfully offer them the expression of our deepest gratitude.

Theodore Trefon
Washington DC
August 2017

GLOSSARY

Alliance of Democratic Forces for the Liberation of Congo-Zaire (AFDL): An anti-Mobutu coalition of dissidents, headed by Laurent-Désiré Kabila, that came to power at the end of the first Congo war (1996–97). The AFDL succeeded in toppling the Mobutu regime but was unable to resolve differences between Kabila and his erstwhile allies (mainly Uganda and Rwanda), which resulted in the outbreak of the second Congo war in August 1998.

Banque Lambert: Congolese euphemism for loan sharking, derived from the name of a Belgian colonial bank.

Banyamulenge: People of South Kivu's mountainous region of Mulenge. A term used to identify ethnic Tutsis of questionable Congolese citizenship.

Birere: A densely populated, bustling commercial district of Goma contiguous to the Rwandan border.

Cassiterite: A derivative of tin ore used in the manufacture of high-tech electronic goods. Fighting over cassiterite deposits in North Kivu has been a major cause of conflict and it is therefore considered a conflict mineral.

Coltan (columbite–tantalite): A metal used in mobile phones, laptop computers and tablets, coltan is mined in the eastern provinces of the DRC and is considered by the US and other governments to be a conflict mineral.

Congolese franc: The franc is the currency of the Democratic Republic of Congo. During the period when we conducted our interviews (2014–15), the exchange rate was approximately 900 francs to one US dollar.

Congolese Institute for Nature Conservation (ICCN): ICCN is responsible for the protection and conservation of the country's network of protected areas, including the Virunga National Park, which is a UNESCO World Heritage Site. ICCN works with various national and international partners.

Congolese Rally for Democracy (RCD): Comprised of numerous factions supported by Rwanda, the RCD was one of the most important Congolese rebel groups operating in eastern DRC before participating in the transitional government formed in June 2003 in the wake of the Sun City Agreement. Its leader, Azarias Ruberwa, became one of the four vice presidents under the 1+4 arrangement (one president, four vice presidents). Created in August 1998 by Ernest Wamba dia Wamba, the RCD seized Goma and launched its attacks against the Kinshasa government, marking the start of the second Congo war. Comprising former AFDL fighters, the RCD was active in combating anti-Tutsi forces in the region. For the Kivu population, brutality and the RCD go hand in hand, in part because of Banyamulenge domination in the RCD.

Gécamines: The Générale des Carrières et des Mines is a partially privatised state-controlled mining giant based in Lubumbashi in the mineral-rich Katanga province. Now largely dismantled, its vast reserves of copper and cobalt made it the economic powerhouse of Congo/ Zaire for decades.

Gomatracien: The name adopted by the inhabitants of Goma, used both in the proper noun and adjectival forms. Others prefer *Goméen*.

Interahamwe: The dominant militia group that perpetrated the massacres of the Rwandan genocide. Established in 1994, Interahamwe signifies 'those who fight together' in Kinyarwanda. Their ideology is Hutu power – Hutu political superiority in Rwanda. Its partisans fled Rwanda – settling in camps of what was then eastern Zaire – following the Rwandan Patriotic Front takeover of Kigali. They joined forces with Hutu soldiers from the former Rwandan Armed Forces in the refugee camps. Opposed to the presidency of Paul Kagame, they formed the Democratic Forces for the Liberation of Rwanda (FDLR) in 2000 to defend Rwandan Hutu interests in the DRC. Efforts to defeat the Interahamwe constituted a partial motivation of Rwanda's involvement in the two Congo wars, whose operations resulted in the death of thousands of former genocide perpetrators and civilians. This poor security situation led to the mass movement of rural populations into zones of perceived greater security, such as the city of Goma.

International Committee of the Red Cross (ICRC): An international humanitarian agency heavily involved in the eastern DRC over the past two decades. It is a neutral and independent institution that assists victims of conflict and armed violence.

Intervention Brigade: A temporary offensive combat force set up by the United Nations in March 2013 to disrupt persistent cycles of violence in the DRC and protect civilians by carrying out targeted operations to neutralise rebel forces, mainly those of the M23 rebellion.

Kadogo: A child soldier. *Kadogos* helped Laurent-Désiré Kabila topple President Mobutu during his march to Kinshasa in 1997. In Swahili, the word means 'still little'.

Khadhafi: An informal street seller of petrol, named after the former Libyan dictator.

M23: The Mouvement du 23 Mars was a group created by Colonel Sultani Makenga in the wake of the Kivu conflicts. Accused of having perpetrated a campaign of violence against civilian communities, the M23 was composed of ex-CNDP rebels, led by Laurent Nkunda, who were reintegrated into the Congolese armed forces according to a peace agreement signed in Kinshasa on 23 March 2009. They mutinied in April 2012 and captured Goma in November 2012. They controlled the city until their defeat in November 2013.

Makala: Lingala and Swahili word for charcoal – the principal source of domestic energy throughout the DRC.

MONUC: The United Nations Organization Mission in the Democratic Republic of the Congo was created by the Security Council in November 1999 to promote a return to peace and stability in the DRC following the signing of the July 1999 Lusaka ceasefire agreement. With more than 20,000 Blue Helmets, MONUC was to become the UN's largest and most expensive operation, with the challenging mandate of participating in the reform of the armed forces and the protection of civilians. The Kivu population believes that the operation has not done enough to protect them, citing the example of the takeover of Bukavu by Laurent Nkunda and Colonel Mutebusi in May and June 2004, when the Blue Helmets remained in their barracks. The Security Council re-baptised MONUC MONUSCO in July 2010.

MONUSCO: The United Nations Organization Stabilization Mission in the Democratic Republic of the Congo replaced MONUC in July 2010. While still mandated to protect civilians, humanitarian personnel and human rights activists, the shift from MONUC to MONUSCO was motivated by the objective of assisting the Congolese government in its efforts at stabilisation and peace-building.

Mutebusi, Jules: Former member of the Rwanda Patriotic Front, Banyamulenge rebel and partisan of the Rassemblement Congolais pour la Démocratie. Accused of numerous war crimes and crimes against humanity, including during the capture of Bukavu with Laurent Nkunda in 2004, he died in Kigali in 2014.

National Commission for Refugees (NCR): The principal governmental partner of the United Nations

High Commission for Refugees in the DRC, based in the Ministry of the Interior. Its main role is registering refugees and internally displaced persons and offering them assistance.

National Congress for the Defence of the People (Congrès National pour la Défense du Peuple or CNDP): A violent armed movement backed by Rwanda, led by Laurent Nkunda. It was heavily involved in the Kivu conflict from 2004 to 2009, fighting against Congolese government forces. The CNDP succeeded in taking control over much of North and South Kivu, causing the displacement of tens of thousands of people, many of whom sought refuge in Goma and Bukavu. In 2009, many of its combatants were integrated into the national army but mutinied once again after a few years, rebranding as the Mouvement du 23 Mars (M23).

Nganga: A word used by many African societies to refer to traditional healers. It is a variation of *munganga*.

Nkunda, Laurent: A Tutsi born in North Kivu. Accused of war crimes, he is being tried by the International Criminal Court in The Hague. In 1993, he joined the Rwandan Patriotic Front, the rebel movement formed by exiled Rwandan Tutsis who came to power after the 1994 Rwandan genocide. In 1998, he was a high-ranking officer in the Rassemblement Congolais pour la Démocratie–Goma (RCD–Goma). He is accused (with General Gabriel Amisi, alias Tango Fort) of the brutal repression of an attempted mutiny in Kisangani in May 2002. Nkunda became a general in the

Congolese national army in 2004 following the 2003 agreement that integrated the RCD into the army. Nkunda refused to take orders from his new hierarchy and fled to South Kivu to combat AFDL *génocidaires* based in eastern DRC. His troops took Bukavu in June 2004 under the pretext of putting an end to the genocide of the Banyamulenges. In September 2005, other Rwandan soldiers who had rallied to the RCD–Goma abandoned the national army to join forces with Nkunda in North Kivu. The Kivu population was traumatised by their actions. Nkunda was arrested in January 2009 in Rwanda, where he had fled to escape from an operation launched against him by a coalition of Congolese and Rwandan forces.

Operation Turquoise: A French-led military operation in Rwanda (from 23 June to 21 August 1994) under the mandate of the United Nations. It is widely perceived as being controversial because of its association with the genocidal Hutu regime and because its mandate undermined another UN peacekeeping force – the United Nations Assistance Mission for Rwanda (UNAMIR).

Raia Mutomboki: Literally 'outraged citizens', this was a self-defence militia that took control of large parts of South Kivu in 2011 to protect people from the abuses of the Democratic Forces for the Liberation of Rwanda (FDLR). Empowered by their belief in witchcraft and supported by local traditional authorities, these 'outraged citizens' mutated into a brutal militia known to have terrorised the people they first sought to protect.

Sun City Agreement: An agreement signed in South Africa on 12 December 2002 marking the beginning of political transition and the gradual end of the second Congo war. It stipulated that Joseph Kabila would share power with four vice presidents – one from each of the two main armed opposition movements, one from the government and one from the unarmed political opposition. Peace-building, political and territorial reunification and the establishment of state control over the country were the stated objectives of this transition, which led to the 2006 presidential and legislative elections. The agreement laid down a political framework and timetable for elections but was not able to end conflict, in part because certain key opposition factions refused to participate.

Tshukudu: A large wooden scooter used to transport heavy loads. The *tshukudu* is a socially important symbol of the city of Goma.

CHRONOLOGY OF EVENTS
IN AND AROUND GOMA

1960 Goma's population is approximately 40,000.

1977 The Nyiragongo volcano erupts on 10 January, killing seventy-two people and destroying property and hundreds of homes.

1987 The former District of North Kivu becomes a new province with Goma as its capital. This puts an end to Goma's political and administrative dependence on Bukavu. Goma's administrative and commercial importance develops rapidly in the wake of this administrative reconfiguration.

1991 Looting sprees take place across the country in September, including in Goma. The already fragile formal economy of the country is destroyed, exacerbating urban poverty and alienating private investors. The looting starts by disgruntled soldiers and turns into a pillaging free-for-all carried out randomly by a frustrated and disenfranchised populace.

1993 A second wave of looting takes place in January and February.

1994 Genocide in Rwanda. From 7 April to 15 July, between 800,000 and 1 million Tutsis and moderate Hutus are massacred in Rwanda. At least 1.2 million refugees arrive in the Kivus, including approximately 100,000 Interahamwe (Hutu militants from Rwanda and Burundi). One million refugees scramble into camps around Goma. Sanitary conditions are catastrophic: in July, 3,000 refugees die daily from inadequate food supplies and a lack of healthcare. The population of North Kivu is traumatised. The genocide leads to ongoing insecurity in the Goma hinterland.

In July, a cholera epidemic breaks out in Goma and the Mugunga, Kibumba and Katale refugee camps, with an estimated 12,000 deaths among the 80,000 people who contract the disease. Humanitarian agencies are overwhelmed and unable to cope with the epidemic – in part because of ill-conceived administrative procedures that limit their mandates.

The American government launches the humanitarian operation Support Hope, based in Goma.

1996 The Alliance of Democratic Forces for the Liberation of Congo-Zaire take Goma in late October with the backing of the Rwandan military. Headed by Ngandu Kisase, the operation is part of the plan to overthrow the Mobutu regime. The end of Kinshasa's domination over the Kivus coincides with commercial and construction booms in Goma.

1997 President Laurent-Désiré Kabila orders the Office of the United Nations High Commissioner for Refugees to leave Goma (and the DRC) on 6 October.

1997–98 The central government loses administrative and political control of the region. Tutsis fill the power vacuum, notably with the advent of the Congolese Rally for Democracy (RCD), a Rwandan proxy and rebel movement led by Wamba dia Wamba.

2002 On 11 January, a Moroccan MONUC Blue Helmet is accused of rape and deported from Goma.
The Nyiragongo volcano erupts on 17 January, destroying between 15 and 20 per cent of the city. Between 350,000 and 500,000 people are displaced. The explosion of a petrol station is the cause of the majority of deaths (approximately 150 people). The eruption sparks a new wave of humanitarian and scientific arrivals.

2003 The Sun City Agreement is signed in South Africa on 19 April but hostilities continue in North Kivu.

2006 The population of Goma suffers sporadic military operations mounted by Rwanda, allegedly to combat Interahamwe forces.

2008 On 23 January, twenty Mai-Mai factions sign a peace agreement with the Congolese government in Goma in the presence of President Joseph Kabila. The plan is to integrate these rebels into the national army.

Amnesty International identifies 224 cases of rape committed by rebels and government soldiers in and around Goma. The report emphasises the vulnerability of the Goma hinterland, which pushes people to seek perceived security in the city.

On 15 April, a Douglas DC-9 aircraft operated by Hewa Bora Airways crashes into the busy Goma neighbourhood of Birere. Approximately seventy passengers and people on the ground lose their lives (the number of victims was never firmly established).

2009 Goma is destabilised by CNDP forces. There is an upsurge in insecurity and targeted assassinations accompanied by the proliferation of heavy weapons in the city.

On 13 March, Albert Ngezayo Prigogine is shot dead in the middle of the day near the Governor's residence. A successful Goma businessman (and nephew of the Belgian Nobel chemistry laureate), he had disagreements with powerful political figures and other business leaders over land ownership.

2010 Emerita Munyashwe, an ally of Laurent Nkunda and supporter of the CNDP, is assassinated on 30 August. It is rumoured that her assassins came from Rwanda.

2012 M23 rebel forces storm the city on 20 November, occupying it for many months. The people of Goma are traumatised by the invasion and disappointed by the central government's powerlessness. Popular uprisings take place against MONUSCO troops who did not intervene and were accused of complicity. Approximately 140,000 people flee Goma during the first few weeks of the occupation, resulting in a renewed wave of major humanitarian assistance. More than 1,000 inmates escape from the Muzenze prison after guards abandon their posts in panic.

2013 The population of Goma is estimated to be 1 million inhabitants.

A Compagnie Africaine d'Aviation (CAA) Fokker 50 aircraft crashes on 4 March, killing five crew members.

The M23 rebel forces are defeated by government troops with the backing of the International Brigade on 7 November.

2014 Funded by the Howard Buffett Foundation, the British actor Jude Law organises a concert with the American performer Akon on the tarmac of Goma airport as part of the International Day of Peace on 21 September.

2015 Clashes on 22 January between the population and security forces take place in the wake of President Kabila's attempt to prolong his mandate, with three casualties.

Members of a Mai-Mai militia attack the airport on 2 June, resulting in seven deaths: four victims from the security forces and three among the attackers.

A joint operation by MONUSCO and government troops is launched in June against the Patriotic Resistance Army of Ituri, resulting in approximately thirty-five deaths.

Ethiopian Airlines inaugurates a regular flight between Addis Abebi and Goma on 14 July. This first international liaison testifies to Goma's commercial potential.

2016 More than 1 million refugees flee civil war in South Sudan in late 2016. Over 530 find refuge in the Munigi camp outside Goma.

2017 In February, the fourth Amani Festival unites more than 34,000 people for three days of music, dance and culture to promote peace in the still wounded North Kivu region.

Rodrigue Mugaruka Katembo is awarded the distinguished Goldman Environmental Prize for Africa for his conservation work in the Virunga National Park.

INTRODUCTION

A CITY IN SEARCH OF ITS FUTURE

GOMA AS RESEARCH SPACE
Theodore Trefon

Suffering, ethnic hatred, poverty and violence are idioms commonly used to describe the social context of Goma and its North Kivu hinterland both by local people and by the swarms of international do-gooders struggling to bring about peace and security. Jealousy, mistrust and fear are other sentiments commonly expressed. For many observers, 'the city is built on conflict'.[1] In her study of perceptions of violence in eastern Congo, Séverine Autesserre relates that the region is often considered as a Hobbesian world of 'war of all against all'.[2] While these quasi-truths cannot be underestimated, in contrast to dominant discourses of violence in which some people have indeed become crazy with brutality, there are also counter-examples of resiliency, pragmatism, balance, freedom and a determination to take charge of one's own destiny. As with many other Congolese cities, there are glimmers of hope in Goma – and patterns of order in the disorder.

This book tells the story of Goma by giving ordinary people a voice. Their quest for well-being and opportunity – as well as their belief in the Lord Almighty and the power of agency – are fundamental drivers that help account for how this bustling city works. Living hell for some, Goma represents promise and opportunity for others. Despite powerlessness and uncertainty, the people of North Kivu's provincial capital express faith through their narratives and provide convincing testimony of universal sentiments in a unique environment where every day is a new challenge. Hardened by adversity where there is no right or wrong, the people we spoke with – haunted by their own night-mares – give the impression that life is neither beautiful nor ugly, but an unending skirmish with destiny. Some tell of victories; others tell of defeat. Some struggle to remember the events of theirs lives; others struggle to forget.

The population of Goma and its hinterland – known and respected for being hard-working – is caught up between several risks: both natural and political. Eruption of the active Nyiragongo volcano, which is located only a few kilometres from the city centre, is a looming threat; the region has a high seismic intensity provoking regular earthquakes; and it has one of the world's highest incidences of lightning strikes. Lake Kivu has an excep-tionally high concentration of underwater methane gas and carbon dioxide. Consequently, it has the potential to explode, reproducing the kind of disaster that happened in Cameroon's Lake Nyos in 1986, killing hundreds of people in a matter of minutes.

The 1994 Rwandan genocide was the single most important tipping point for those living in the city and its environs. With 800,000 dead in Rwanda and 2,000,000 refugees, it changed the entire complexion of the region. Its enduring impact has been social, political, economic, ethnic, demographic and environmental.

The lack of electricity, water, health and education infrastructures – and reliable administrative service provision – exacerbates the trials and tribulations of these men, women and children who seem accustomed to hardship. The problems of Goma's people are therefore real and apparently sustainable, which is why they say that 'temporary solutions have become permanent'. Interviews with Goma's youth produced a similar observation: the state of emergency has become normal.[3]

The population is also struggling with an unresolved identity crisis. *Kinois*, *Lushois* and *Boyomais* are the names adopted by the inhabitants of Kinshasa, Lubumbashi and Kisangani respectively. What do the people of Goma call themselves? *Gomatraciens* and *Goméens* are their nicknames, but people have not enthusiastically embraced either one. It is likewise curious that Goma is one of the few large Congolese cities today that was not given a European name. Perhaps the settlement was not considered sufficiently prestigious to be associated with the Belgian royal family (Leopoldville, Elizabethville, Albertville ...), military heroes (Coquilhatville, Costermansville), businessmen (Thysville) or explorers (Stanleyville) or to deserve such a name in the minds of the colonial administration.

This book – in which people's stories intermingle with our analysis, observations and comments – is the first urban sociology of this unsettling danger-fraught social crucible. It is based on a subjective and personalised approach that enables readers to discover the intimate feelings of the population and the multiple realities they grapple with on a daily basis. Grounded in twelve life stories, we attempted to establish a balance between young and old, informal and formal sector workers, women and men, the educated and less educated. Indeed, the way in which people perceive danger and well-being is influenced by these factors of age, gender, level of education, economic activity, place of residence and family history. The relationships between social networking and individual striving is a recurring theme in the trajectories of those featured in the book. *Goma: Stories of strength and sorrow* aims to tell the stories in a humanising way, giving a voice to the agents of Goma's ongoing search for identity.

Goma has not been studied much by researchers (its bibliography is short compared with the lengthy list of works devoted to other Congolese cities, such as Kinshasa or Lubumbashi) but it has been studied fairly well – notably over the past fifteen years. Research themes include demographic growth and spatial expansion, Goma as a border town, humanitarian aid delivery, Goma as a city of refuge, ethnic mobilisation and urban identity.[4] The most comprehensive study of Goma is Karen Büscher's doctoral dissertation (which I co-supervised with Koen Vlassenroot), in which she describes the

process of urban development and social transformation since the city's establishment a century ago in the
double context of regional violence and state failure.[5]
Her analysis, like the work of most other researchers
focusing on Goma, highlights the opportunities – real
and imagined – the city has to offer.

The Pole Institute, which is based in Goma, is a peace-
building and research institution that regularly tracks the
city's socio-political context. Their research and aware-
ness-building activities extend beyond the city limits,
taking into account regional dynamics. Hundreds of
non-governmental organisations (NGOs) and humanitarian agencies headquartered in Goma also produce
reports, primarily concerning regional security issues but
sometimes about specific urban issues.

The juxtaposition between Goma and its hinterland
is an unavoidable research consideration. From social,
spatial and economic perspectives, it is difficult to say
where the city ends and where rural life begins. They are
not distinct spaces because both urban and rural traits
marry, forming one vast human geography. This overlapping explains why we included in our selection of social
universes activities that are not strictly urban – the bean
and *makala* trade, for example, coffee production and the
tshukudu's vital role in urban food supply. This kind of
overlapping exists with Rwanda too ('land of the brothers
we don't like'), notably with respect to the bustling trade
between Goma and Gisenyi (the Rwandan town on the
border). Massive resettlement of Banyarwanda (children

of Rwanda) in the Kivus, starting after World War I and subsequently encouraged by Belgian colonial planners in the 1930s, was an important historical policy, the impact of which continues to be narrated today by the people of Goma.

Genocide, war, militia activity and other forms of conflict have undeniably contributed to the making of the Goma of today. The extraction of coltan and cassiterite, the region's main conflict minerals, has also had an impact. To fully understand the social dynamics of the city presented in the following stories, it is useful to consider Goma in the broader historical, regional and political economy context. This contextualisation exercise, however, is beyond the scope of our ambitions here; there is no need to rehash what others have already done. A number of studies in English and French have presented this background, mainly by drawing on political science analysis.[6] A survey into perceptions of fear in eastern Congo was carried out by Patrick Vinck et al.,[7] and Georges Berghezan and Xavier Zeebroek produced a similar study on perceptions of insecurity.[8] A few journalistic accounts written in the first person are available as well – those by Justine Brabant et al. and Ben Rawlence, for example.[9]

TELLING STORIES

The piecing together of personal narratives is a powerful research approach that is well suited to understanding people's innermost thoughts and beliefs. What people declare – or choose not to declare – about their personal trajectories and their discourses are rarely strictly individual. Their narratives reflect contemporary slices of lived collective history. Narratives are therefore more than the sum of their parts – they are threads in a complex social fabric.[10] Often these threads converge; sometimes they diverge; and in some instances they appear inextricably jumbled. In the case of Goma and the traumatising dynamics of the region, the following stories confirm these observations. Some views are shared by our interviewees, others are contradicted. Even within individual narratives – those of Papy or Mathilde, for example – inherent contradictions are obvious.

The book's format, based on a culturally sensitive approach, portrays eastern Congo in an engaging and accessible way, allowing real people to speak about their ordinary and extraordinary experiences. We have used information derived from in-depth interviews and participatory observation to explain some of the dominant social universes that shape the city. The experiences described by our interviewees, who reveal wide-ranging social diversity, are both shared and disputed by thousands of other people in the city and the region.

The DRC is known for its poor data collection, unreliable reporting and lack of precision. Popular voices, therefore, help fill the data vacuum. Although quantitative studies are not superfluous, they are unable to make sense of social dynamics at the individual, family, neighbourhood and community levels. Social science researchers and humanitarian agencies have come to accept that analysis

based on qualitative studies is necessary to validate quantitative surveys – but the size of the research sample
remains subject to debate. We could easily have added
more narratives in this collection – stories from money
changers (*cambistes*), street-level petrol sellers (*khadhafis*),
mineral traders, waste collectors, preachers, unregulated
pharmacists, hotel and restaurant workers, and teachers,
to name only a few. However, in a city the size of Goma, it
was necessary to select. We responded to the question of
the ideal number of stories with another one: how many
stories are needed to establish sociological truth? It seems
obvious that neither quantity nor artificial demands of
representativeness matter. This is just one unique set of
amazing stories – so, to paraphrase Rosario Giordano, a
city of 1 million inhabitants translates into 1 million life
histories.[11] These individual stories clearly help portray
the broader story of the city.

Our ambition, therefore, was to tell stories of universal
interest amidst this idiosyncratic social environment. Even
though this qualitative storytelling does not pretend to
fall into the category of applied policy work, I contend
that an understanding of social dynamics is a prerequisite
for elaborating the myriad development strategies being
implemented on behalf of the Congolese authorities by civil
society organisations and international financial partners.

THE CAST OF CHARACTERS

Below is a brief introduction to the people with whom
we have worked and their social universes. The aim is

to let readers quickly identify the stories they may find most appealing or pertinent to their own interests. The sequencing of the stories in the book is random: we decided not to settle on 'the' most coherent order because multiple ways of presenting them make sense. They could have been grouped by gender to emphasise the determination of women in taking charge of their destinies, or by economic activities to highlight the dynamism of the informal sector. Some stories are focused solely on the city while others trace the relations between Goma and its hinterland. Some individuals in this collection, moreover, are quite simply nicer or more sympathetic than others. Is Cerezo the *tshukudeur* more representative of Goma than Asumani the motorbike taxi driver, or Doctor Chantal Sasolele compared with Bernadette the market woman? Probably not: all of them are pieces making up the social puzzle of Goma, contributing to how and why the city is the way it is today – and what it may become tomorrow. The stories can therefore be read in the order they appear, but readers can also wander through them led by their own curiosity.

Mathilde Musole is a surprising businesswoman who has run the gauntlet personally and professionally in a city she sees as one of commercial opportunity. She can best be described as energetic, enterprising and shrewd. In her description of her life as mother and father, cabaret owner and trader with Dubai, church-going social climber and loan shark, her story resounds with her determination to take charge of her own destiny and provide for her offspring. From selling doughnuts on the street as a young mother to selling high-tech gadgets as an established trader today, her experience is firmly embedded in Goma's economic dynamism. She says that her own story, like that of Goma, is 'incomplete'.

The ingeniously designed *tshukudu* competes with the Nyiragongo volcano as Goma's most emblematic symbol. While the emergence of this handmade wooden scooter could be considered an inventive popular response to transportation and employment needs, it could also be considered a reminder of underdevelopment in the Congo. Cerezo's narrative testifies to the dynamism, creativity and solidarity of the hundreds of *tshukudeurs* who have become indispensable in trolleying building supplies, produce, furniture and other loads that in other cities would be hauled by lorry. Every few days, Cerezo shuttles between his peri-urban farm and Goma with vegetables for a restaurant that caters to the city's middle class and expatriate aid community. His dream is to help his children become fully fledged city dwellers who can 'enjoy water from a tap' and other urban amenities. 'The city may modernise,' he says, 'but the population will depend on my rudimentary *tshukudu* for years to come.'

Few households in the DRC have electricity and Goma is no exception (although low-capacity solar installations are increasingly visible on rooftops). Most households consequently rely on charcoal for cooking. The charcoal business is therefore an economic opportunity but one that comes with a high environmental impact, notably because most of Goma's charcoal comes from Africa's oldest nature reserve – the emblematic Virunga National Park. Exiled Hutu refugees from Rwanda (former *génocidaires* and their offspring) control much of its production and lucrative trade. Nguba Liboko, who miraculously survived a cholera epidemic that wiped out his entire family on Idjwi Island in Lake Kivu when he was a child, is a charcoal wholesaler. He was previously involved with partners in charcoal production and transport so knows the intricacies of the entire supply chain and the actors he has to negotiate with along the way. After having survived skirmishes with Mai-Mai rebels and M23 troops, he says he thanks God for his relative good fortune.

Goma would not be Goma without the Nyiragongo volcano. Eruption is a permanent threat. The last two major eruptions (1977 and 2002) destroyed property and took lives. People who experience an eruption never forget it. But there are some advantages too: indeed, the city is built largely with lava stones – mainly for house foundations and walls. And lava and volcanic ash also make for fertile soil. Celestin and Mituga are two friends who, with their rudimentary tools and steel-like biceps, have learned to 'discipline' the lava into useful building blocks. Forlorn and poor, they have accepted their lot in life, saying: 'We've stopped dreaming about a better tomorrow; we've learned to do without.' Their joint narrative provides insightful information about the haves and the have-nots, house building and urban crawl without urban planning.

The health sector in Goma is confronted by a singular set of constraints resulting from regional violence and a vulnerable population's stressful struggle to survive. It is a hybrid sector with ultramodern hospitals funded by foreign partners, a dilapidated public health delivery system, small private clinics and traditional healers. The pragmatic Doctor Chantal Sasolele describes how patients 'shop around' depending on the type of care needed and how much money can be scraped together. Trust in Western medical science and belief in witchcraft is jumbled in her consultations with patients. Doctor Chantal reveals with empathy the defeats and suffering of her patients but also their victories and hopes. Her account of the worst day of her life as a doctor is a powerful social commentary.

The population of eastern DRC has gone through one of the twenty-first century's worst social tragedies. Goma has become the principal hub for hundreds of humanitarian agencies and NGOs – but ones that are hampered by unrealistic mandates, poor coordination and, sometimes, conflicting agendas. Their presence over the years has transformed the socio-economic condition of the city through, for example, the employment of staff, the house and office rental market and indirect service provision. Eric Kyungu went from being a hotel bookkeeper to a humanitarian professional employed by the Red Cross. Eric is an active member of a Catholic congregation. His sardonic analysis of Goma's humanitarian 'business' is based on sentiments of cynicism, altruism and opportunism.

Beans are intimately associated with local identity. They are all over the city: in fields, in kitchen gardens, and, of course, in pots simmering over smoky charcoal fires. Buying and selling them is a means for women like Bernadette Mpunga to sustain a modest lifestyle and achieve social recognition. The busy market where she has her stand is full of life and drama. Wife and mother by the time she was seventeen, she has been able to find peace of mind in Goma thanks to her hard work. Nevertheless, she remains wary of the 'malicious spirits' that could wreak havoc in her household and workplace. Humble, she considers herself part of the 'insignificant multitude'. While relating her story, Bernadette also describes administrative issues at the market, security problems in the Goma hinterland (where her husband buys beans wholesale) and transportation logistics.

The roar of the motorbike taxi is one of Goma's characteristic sounds. This means of getting around, now widespread throughout the DRC, started in Goma as cheap Chinese and Indian motorbikes became available via East Africa. As the city became increasingly spread out, new transportation needs emerged. The motorbike taxi is cost-efficient for passengers and provides work for unskilled young men with relatively low entry costs. It would be impossible to fully grasp Goma's social landscape without looking at the motorbike's role. Asumani Birewa had to leave school at a young age when his father died, and he then floated from job to job in his village in Masisi. He later settled in Goma, hoping to find office work, but, he recalls, 'My big brother's promises were unrealistic – he didn't have the pull to get me hired.' He eventually seized upon the opportunity of becoming a motorbike taxi driver, which he took: 'It was better than nothing.' He describes Goma through his experience with traffic police, passengers, fellow drivers and mechanics. His universe is the motorbike – for both work and leisure.

Insecurity in eastern Congo has created new needs for private security companies, of which there are dozens in Goma today, catering to the protection of well-to-do Congolese and expatriate humanitarian and development workers. The companies recruit former soldiers and militia members – many of whom have blood on their hands, such as Papy Bahati. His story intertwines his experience as a drifter with the recent military history of the country. He tells his story according to military events that affected his life, such as Laurent-Désiré Kabila's break with his Rwandan and Ugandan backers, battles in Kisangani, a 'mistaken' deportation to Rwanda and rebellion in South Kivu. He admits that his work as a private security agent is politically dubious but insists that 'having a clear conscience is a luxury for somebody like me', particularly in an unpredictable environment where 'it is cheaper to buy a Kalashnikov than a goat'. Papy is an eternal malcontent who sees himself as a predestined victim, with the need to be constantly looking over his shoulder. He considers that randomness and accident – not justice – have defined his life.

Isabelle Michel is a Belgian agronomist who has spent most of her working life in the Congo, mainly as a coffee plantation manager for the past twenty-five years. As her plantation lies in the immediate Goma hinterland, she is an excellent source of information about how the city has evolved. The plantation's uninterrupted production is a surprising example of commercial resiliency in a conflict zone, and it requires the maintenance of good relations with a host of actors. She describes Goma's social, economic, spatial and security changes since she first discovered what has become her second home. Concerned with the well-being of the plantation's hundreds of workers and proud to participate in the 'noble enterprise' of getting coffee into our cups, this white European woman with a deep attachment to Congo and the Congolese admits that 'going to bed in Belgium without locking the door, worrying about the volcano or being attacked is some-times a welcome relief'.

Even though most of Goma's economy is informal, there are also formal sector activities. Martin Mboma runs the provincial office of the Federation of Congolese Enter-prise, whose mandate is to promote and facilitate private investment while also serving as a link between compa-nies and government. His narrative helps us understand how the informal and formal sectors converge to make Goma a bustling city of opportunity. Martin offers an unexpected account of officialdom because, even in the context of weak state structures, the Federation contrib-utes to the economic dynamism of Goma. His advice to potential investors (from fruit juice prospectors to hotel developers) reflects his personal trajectory: 'Only the paranoid survive – and only the really paranoid prosper.' His message is similar to those of many Goma residents: 'Never underestimate the power of a relationship.'

Goma is a rapidly changing city, and a young one too. Approximately half of its inhabitants are under eighteen years old. To understand the dynamics of change, therefore, listening to how the young express their expectations, determination and frustrations is unavoidable. Many youths are disoriented, having been broken by uncertainty, politics, conflict and family trauma. They have to grow up quickly. There is, however, in addition to those who complain of seeing little hope for the future, a category of gilded young adults. Clarisse Soki is one of them. With a degree from the University of Goma, she has a busy social life, a comfortable family home, a new car, plans for work and leisure, and a sense of her own importance. While she is the first to admit that she was born under a lucky star, she also realises that her conveniences are petty and her self-satisfaction is illusory.

ENTANGLED SOCIAL REALITIES

Common themes emerge when engaging with the people of Goma. It is obvious that security concerns and money worries are their main preoccupations, surpassing by far the fear of volcanic eruption. People even say that they are used to the plume of the Nyiragongo, referring to it as their 'neighbour' or 'big brother'. Is volcanic activity, moreover, a natural risk or a supernatural one? The response is ambiguous in many minds and there is no obvious answer. The last eruption took place on 17 January 2002 – a date permeated with connotation. The population of Goma are far from insensitive to the fact that national hero Patrice Lumumba was killed on a 17 January (1961) and Laurent-Désiré Kabila on 16 January a half century later (2001).

The fear of militia fighters, government soldiers, common bandits and assassins is in everyone's discourse. These security problems became apparent in the imme-diate aftermath of the Rwandan genocide, exacerbating pre-existing threats from predatory soldiers – an enduring legacy of the Mobutu dictatorship. The people of Goma appear cautious and suspicious because of these real threats, which also help account for their general lack of light-heartedness. 'We go to bed early because danger lurks more in the dark than in daylight' – a common-sense reaction that indicates how people adapt to their environ-ment as best they can. People undoubtedly have good reason to be afraid but their fear needs to be nuanced. Martin Mboma, who describes his city as a 'strange place of unanswered questions', provides a subtle twist: 'Danger is all over and when problems come, there will be victims – but there will be survivors too.'

Mathilde Musole has encapsulated what many of her friends and neighbours feel about household finances: 'You can't be happy without financial security.' Before this can be achieved, however, most voices converge to say that you must persevere, know how to adapt and learn quickly – in addition to being a little bit lucky. 'Wicked spirits, witchcraft and evil spells,' according to Bernadette Mpunga, are forces to avoid in the fight against adversity. She therefore does whatever she can not to give her potential adversaries reason to be jealous. The people of Goma rarely use the term 'resilience' but they have multiple expressions to express it: 'stick to it', 'get up when you have been knocked down', 'fend for yourself', 'do the impossible', 'learn from your mistakes' and 'face up to reality', for example.

The importance of education is another common theme uppermost in people's discourse. While many people in Goma survive on the margins of the law, inventing new tricks to beat the system (because 'it isn't fair if we can't cheat'), they pray to God for help in finding and keeping 'real' work. Education and a diploma 'help one stand above the others' and are perceived as being a key to the door of recruitment. Like other parents who 'did not wear out the seat of his trousers on a school bench', Cerezo the *tshukudeur* has high hopes for his children to become 'educated city dwellers'. Doctor Chantal Sasolele adds another perspective on education: 'Insecurity, mobility and the general deterioration of state services have taken a heavy toll on children's education. It is a problem that contributes to our vulnerability.'

The unfulfilled role of the state is a frequently heard complaint, particularly with respect to its abdication in safeguarding physical security. The population is also very sensitive to the state's ability to do harm, in addition to which 'state agents are so present but so useless'. Somewhat less obvious is the perception of a gap between the economic dynamism of the city and the absence of state services, pointing to the population's capacity to get things done through their own commercial and solidarity networks. Infrastructure deficiencies, as elsewhere throughout the country, are high on the list of complaints. 'The absence of running water is the big scandal of Goma,' insists Isabelle Michel: 'It is a real social tragedy.'

The absence of a functioning state is a direct cause of the strong presence of humanitarian aid in Goma. Humanitarian agencies and NGOs have replaced the state – at the same time handicapping its ability to regain sovereignty. Consequently, 'humanitarian aid helps but destabilises at the same time'. While the dream of many skilled people, such as Clarisse Soki and Eric Kyungu, is to work in the sector, they realise that it also 'artificially boosts the economy' and that there will be a 'devastating void' when the humanitarians leave. With a view from the inside, Eric – who is an altruistic sceptic – is well placed to analyse the humanitarian sector's relative inefficiency.

References to God and prayer (*Mungu na maombi*), religion in general and other belief systems are omnipresent in people's stories. Trust and mistrust in providence overlap. Papy Bahati looks to the Lord to reinforce his hope of improving his human condition and because 'God is the best defence to ward off adversity'. Looking back over the years, Martin Mboma does not waver in his conviction that 'it is only thanks to the Almighty that I have been able to avoid the traps destiny has laid for me'. After having narrowly escaped an ambush from M23 fighters, Liboko the charcoal trader 'glories the Eternal' for leaving him safe and sound. The Lord is undoubtedly a major force in the lives of the people of Goma but it is not because he traces their destinies that they will not do the 'physically unthinkable and morally repugnant' to get ahead. The ambiguity between the belief that events are predestined and the will to take charge of one's existence is a striking sociological phenomenon in this city of false refuge where life goes on but where the future remains uncertain.

CHAPTER 1

THE UPS AND DOWNS
OF A BUSINESSWOMAN

A SCHOOL GIRL ESCAPES
FORCED MARRIAGE

Mathilde Musole is an independent-minded business-woman with pluck. Clever, hard-working and tenacious – like the city of Goma – her life has been a rollercoaster ride of ups and downs. Her indefatigable drive to take charge of her destiny, her resiliency in the face of adversity and her near-permanent smile are her dominant personality traits. Most people call her Aunty Mathy, Da Mathy (*da* is short for *dada*, which is the Swahili word for sister) or Mama Teacher. With multiple irons in the fire, she is not easily intimidated by hard work or the need to think creatively.

Mathilde was born into a Bashi family on 28 December 1963 in a small village near Bukavu in South Kivu, the second to last child of eight. Her parents did not send her older sisters to school because they considered their future to be that of wife and mother. 'Girls learn to take care of a household in our family – not waste their time in class. In my case, however, my father changed his mind.'

When she was four years old, her father (a cook for priests in a Catholic mission) and her mother (a market woman) decided to send her to live with an older sister in Bukavu so she could go to school. The quality of teaching in the city was significantly better than in her native village. 'I studied hard and finished primary school without any difficulty and then followed a teacher-training curriculum in boarding school at the Lycée des Sœurs Noires in Katana near Bukavu.'

Over the years, Mathilde would return to her village to visit her parents. 'One summer – I was fifteen and pretty – my father accepted to marry me off. The suitor paid the traditional dowry of two cows for my hand but agreed to wait until I finished school to finalise the marriage.' Upon graduation in 1981, Da Mathy made it clear to her father that she did not want anything to do with her fiancé: 'Schoolgirls shouldn't be forced to marry,' she argued. She had in fact made her own plans with another young man, François, also a Shi and a trained nurse. Her father reluctantly came to accept her choice and offered to return the two cows to the jilted fiancé. 'He withdrew his claim on me but for reasons that I never understood, he refused to take back the dowry.'

Mathilde learned to like studying as a high school student and dreamed of going to university in Kinshasa. 'I had the talent to succeed but my dream was put on hold for want of money.' In the meantime, and with the intention of putting money aside for further studies, she worked as a statistics analyst in the provincial administration of primary, secondary and professional education (EPSP) in Bukavu. François was anxious to get married but Mathilde's older brothers did not agree, preferring to see their little sister continue her education. Despite their veto, the young couple went ahead with their marriage and rented a house in Bukavu where Mathilde continued to work. Her first setback took the form of sexual harassment by her boss at work: she quit and took a job as a primary school teacher in the Bukavu district of Ibanda. 'That's where I got the name Mama Teacher that has stuck with me all these years.'

CONQUERING POVERTY

Despite bringing home two salaries, the young couple was quickly confronted by the difficulties of making ends meet when their first daughter was born. The Zairian economy was in a tailspin as a result of hyperinflation, low levels of investment, decaying infrastructure, corruption and low salaries. Two years into their marriage, François needed to come up with a plan, so he decided to go back to school. He enrolled at the Butare branch of the National University of Rwanda to study pharmacology, leaving his wife and daughter behind. He shuttled back and forth between Butare and Bukavu for three years, a phase during which Mathilde continued to teach. After graduating, François found work in a pharmaceutical trading company in Gitarama, Rwanda, and a year later, in 1987, he was promoted and transferred to Gisenyi – the Rwandan city just opposite Goma. Mathilde was able to arrange for a transfer from Bukavu to Goma, where the reunited couple settled.

> Goma at the time was still a small city whose activities were centred around the newly constructed international airport, catering to the expanding tourist business, the main attraction being the Virunga park. As an inexperienced schoolteacher coming from a sleepy administrative town, I was dazzled by the fancy hotels – Grands Lacs, Mont Goma and the Ritz. I nagged François to take me out dancing in fashionable nightclubs Saturday nights, basking in the pleasure of my new environment. I loved going to bustling Birere on weekdays to do my shopping. I can't forget how impressed I was by the *khadhafis* who weaved in and out of the labyrinth of busy alleyways – allegedly so dangerous to the uninitiated.

Salaries in Congo/Zaire tend to be lower than those in neighbouring countries. With the money François was earning in Rwanda, he was able to buy a motorbike to commute between Gisenyi and Goma. The motorbike was an indicator of the couple's improved standard of living. Likewise, François conceded that he was earning enough money to cover the household expenses and pressured Mathilde to stop teaching: 'A wife who has children to bring up shouldn't work.' A year's worth of savings allowed the couple to buy a large plot of land in Himbi, where they planned to build their house. They thus participated in the first postcolonial expansion of Goma – at the time, Himbi was mostly vacant land with a few cultivated fields. 'Compared to today, prices were insignificant. In 1988, we bought 3,200 square metres of land for 150 Zaires [around $80].'

Mathilde took responsibility for negotiating the purchase. In 2014 she sold an eighth of the land for $10,000, which testifies to the inflation in land prices. In 1990, as the area where they had their land was becoming urbanised, it was again Mathilde who took charge of validating their ownership, first with the neighbourhood officials and then with the municipal land title office. Although she did the best she could to preserve the full size of their lot, she was unsuccessful. 'For a little bit of land, people will do anything. I had to give up part of the lot to keep the peace. Our future neighbours got some but most went to the agent at the land title office. I wasn't too upset because I thought that maybe he could help me down the road.'

Once they were in possession of their title, they built their house of wooden planks, typical of the Goma style of housebuilding. Mathilde oversaw the construction, allowing François to concentrate on his work. 'We were delighted to say goodbye to our landlord and move into our own place. Without having to worry about rent, we were able to furnish the house with expensive things. Thanks to our ingrained savings mentality, we could fulfil another dream – shared by everyone from South Kivu – buy a house in Bukavu – which in our case was a second residence.' It took them two more years of saving but the little brick house in the nice residential area of Ibanda in Bukavu was theirs. 'For Bashi people like us, owning a home in Bukavu means that we have conquered poverty!' Today, however, Da Mathy admits that she would not leave Goma for Bukavu because Goma presents far more 'tempting business opportunities'.

Mathilde convinced her husband to allow her to start work again, arguing that she knew how to space out her pregnancies. She hired a young Hunde boy to take care of domestic chores so she could 'pick up the chalk' once again. 'Being with children and having them call me Mama Teacher filled me with pride.' She recommenced in a public school (the Tuungane Institute) and then taught at a better-paying private primary school (Les Volcans), where she stayed from 1987 to 1995. 'As in many other Congolese families, the money I earned was mine – François' money was ours – to spend on living expenses. He agreed I could do what I wanted with my money so I put it in a savings cooperative.'

They were not rich during those years but comfortably off: neither parents nor children felt deprived. 'We had everything we needed and couldn't see any dark clouds on the horizon – but then lightning struck.' In January 1995, François died suddenly from kidney failure. 'I was devastated by his death.' A paternal aunt from Bukavu took in her oldest son, but no one in the family helped her with the other three children. 'I had to adapt, forced into playing the double role of mama and papa.' Her first concern was to maintain a material standing of living comparable to the one they had before François died.

'I needed to find work that paid better and got lucky with a teaching job at the Belgian school in September 1995. That job allowed me to keep the kids well dressed and well fed while keeping the house up. I was even able to save each month, putting something in the savings and credit cooperative.' Her children were allowed to study at the Belgian school too, something she was grateful for. Maintaining this rhythm, however, came at a high cost: 'I worked liked a dog!' For two years, 1995 and 1996, she got up at 5 am to prepare her lessons and get the children dressed, washed and fed. 'I knew that I had to be demanding with myself if I was to avoid losing my job.'

This struggle lasted until February 1996 – when the Democratic Forces for the Liberation of the Congo entered Goma. As the rebels came, the expatriates fled – including the Belgians. Before leaving, the Belgian school director asked Mathilde, along with the Tutsi father of a student at the school, to take over the interim management during what proved to be a hectic transition. The school's finances suffered as students left, and this had a direct impact on Mathilde's salary. 'To make matters worse, my co-manager did not hide the fact that he expected me to become his mistress. My refusal led to further problems because he was able to push me out of my management responsibilities and take full control of the school.' Mathilde maintained her teaching job temporarily but the stress of being sexually harassed and the worry about being sacked led her to have a nervous breakdown. This was the beginning of another period of precariousness because she was not paid during the two months of her hospitalisation. Her attempts at receiving compensation were fruitless and her fear about being sacked came true. 'This experience didn't do much to improve my opinion of our Tutsi neighbours.'

Without any source of income, Mathilde had to start again from scratch, realising that her savings would not last long. She decided to take a chance and bought a stock of used shoes to sell. 'I didn't know anything about the used-shoe market but was able to see how other women were organised. It was not very complicated.' Nevertheless, the earnings did not reach her expectations and she abandoned that trade. Her next commercial venture was selling fresh milk and street food. 'Every morning, I'd get up before 5 am and walk over to Gisenyi with my 20 litre jug and walk back home with it full of milk. I wasn't going to waste money on a motorbike taxi! By 6 am, I would be back at the house mixing doughnut dough and deep-frying it on my little *brasero*.' Once the doughnuts were ready, she would wake up her daughters who would sell them on a make-shift table in front of the house – along with a few other items such as sugar, candy, spices and soap. During that time, she would be selling the milk door to door. Although the family was making ends meet with these activities, Mathilde became aware that the rhythm was having a negative impact on the girls' school results. The energetic widow consequently transitioned into yet another venture.

This time it was selling used clothing, an important business in Africa that exists because of donations from Europe and America. The idea came to her thanks to advice given by some friends from Bukavu, where the trade first developed in the region. 'My girlfriends and I would pool our money to buy large loads of used clothing imported via the Kenyan port of Mombasa. There was a lot of solidarity between us in terms of sharing costs and divvying up earnings and in selecting who wanted what from the stock.' Her acumen for the business came easily as she learned by doing, focusing on four categories of clients and goods. The first category comprised 'nearly new' items that she would sell to priests and sisters from the approximately fifty Catholic congregations in and around Goma. 'I liked doing business with them because they didn't quibble over prices.' Second were items in decent condition she would display at the Virunga market; third, loads she would sell in bundles to buyers from neighbouring villages who would in turn sell them item by item. Last were wholesale bundles she would take to Sake on market days for either sale or barter for foodstuffs (beans, cabbage, potatoes, and so on) that she would sell in Goma for a profit. The used clothing chapter in her life was successful and she was able to hire a seller for her stand in the Virunga market and a housekeeper to take care of domestic chores.

Driven by a mix of ambition and a fear of relapsing into poverty, Mathilde used her second-hand clothing earnings to invest in a bar, which, thanks to her many friends and acquaintances, attracted a large clientele.

Located on a busy street near the Himbi II goat market,
she served food and drink on an array of white plastic
tables. 'I had a big freezer that kept the beer nice and cold.
My guests could sit out on the front terrace if they wanted
to watch the passers-by; others could enjoy the discretion
of private rooms behind the main courtyard. There were
always chicken parts, fish and pork on the charcoal grill to
accompany the beer.' After a while she also invested in a
sound and light system for a little discotheque space. 'I had
both regular customers and plenty of one-time visitors.'
Based on her success and public relations shrewdness,
Mathilde convinced Bralima (one of the major breweries)
to grant her an exclusivity contract, which boosted her bar
business. Most importantly, Mathilde was able to exploit
the arrangement to sell Bralima products wholesale. She
combined this with beer and alcohol imports from Bujumbura, Kampala and Dar es Salaam. 'The fear of being poor
again had dissipated. No more young widow remorse for
me – I had become a real businesswoman.'

The spirit of financial independence gave Mathilde the
confidence to take control of her sentimental affairs. She
admits that 'masculine tenderness' is a welcome thing
after years of solitude but is clear with respect to her
suitors' intentions: 'Men chase after me because they want
to get their hands on my money. I give in now and again
but pick and choose. I don't want anything to do with a
man who is either rude or domineering.' Her choice leans
towards men who are 'tender, committed, thoughtful,
caring and ready to cater to my whims'. Even when she

has happened upon such a man, she remains adamantly opposed to remarriage. Independence is a priority and she insists that she would not want anyone 'to boast that they have contributed a single iota to my accomplishments'.

PREDATORS NEVER DIE

Da Mathy, like most other Congolese citizens, is subject to the demands of civil servants and other types of state agents. When she put together the file for her first job, her marriage certificate, the birth certificates of her children, and the land title were just a few examples of the requirements that initiated her into the idiosyncrasies of local administrative reality.

> I figured out quickly that you have to deal with the boss in the back office – not the clerk that does the leg work or sits at the window. When possible, I've avoided even going into a public service office because once you get in, you are like a mouse between the claws of a hungry cat. Those guys pretend to be so busy that helping you would be a major inconvenience; they make you feel guilty and helpless at the same time. Even after you have emptied your wallet, there are no guarantees that you are going to leave with the paper you went in for. To avoid all this, my strategy entails establishing friendly relations with the big men.

To do so, she invites them to her bar and gives them beer and food – 'just enough to open the conversation and get their phone numbers'. Once they get to know each other better, she asks for favours in getting the necessary papers approved or in getting their lower echelon workers 'off my back'. Through this relatively innocuous form of manipulation, Mathilde avoids paying for some services, or at least pays a smaller amount than would be expected. 'It isn't possible to get off for free all the time but I know how to cut my losses with these predators who never die.'

Mathilde has a long list of administrative requirements she has had to deal with over the years. To sell clothes at the Virunga market she had to pay an entrance fee, a fee for a display table (even though her goods were sold on tarpaulin sheets on the ground) and a daily market tax. She had no fewer than five agents 'poking their nose in my business' for her bar and wholesale alcohol depot. The municipality issued the authorisation to start the business and the annual licence. The income service (DGI) sent agents to collect fees required by small companies employing staff. Another tax agency (the DGRAD) had its own agents collect tax ostensibly for the same reasons. Agents from the environmental services also came with a checklist of conditions; the department of hygiene, which verified the cleanliness of the establishment, followed. Before connecting the water and electricity meters, the Regideso and SNEL needed to receive their envelopes. For her business trips beyond Congo's borders, there are requirements that need to be met with the immigration services (DGM) – a kind of exit visa – and with the customs and excise tax collectors (DGDA) for import–export activities. Mathilde's assessment of this is pragmatic: 'These are things you have to do to stay in business. I'm grateful that I have the savvy to figure things out.'

THE DOUBLE LIFE OF A SOCIAL CLIMBER

With her busy work agenda and responsibilities at home, it is hard to see how Mathilde has any time for a social life. But she does. 'I'm active in a women's association caring for widows who were not as lucky as me.' Members meet informally, sharing information, giving advice and exchanging opinions. The association has a small rotating credit system for members in need. 'I am also active in the Beke girls' association for Bukavu women living in Goma. We meet every other Sunday at one of the members' house for what we call kitchen parties.' Behind the fabricated image of a generous and socially engaged woman lies a pragmatic, no-nonsense entrepreneur who does not take her business arrangements lightly. Mathilde Musole is also a loan shark – lending money at very high interest rates. 'We call this Banque Lambert. It is a tough business with its ups and downs – just like any other money-making enterprise. Sometimes you work with honest customers and make money; sometimes with crooks who screw you.'

A customs officer asked for a $1,000 loan to pay for his son's tuition in Kampala. Even before the approach of the agreed thirty-day deadline he paid me the principal and interest – $1,500. Two months later he needed

$2,000, which I readily agreed to lend because of his respect of the previous deal. He seemed trustworthy and did indeed reimburse my money on schedule. A few months later he asked me for $3,000. I didn't have that much cash on hand and had to borrow it myself but at a slightly lower rate than I charged him. Two weeks after the deadline I didn't hear from him and my calls went unanswered. I waited a couple more weeks and then finally went to his house to collect. His wife opened the door and welcomed me with threats and insults. I had to run to escape a beating. With the interest that he owes, it would be impossible to pay back even for a dishonest customs officer. I had to cover the loss and move ahead with other deals – and there are plenty of entries in my little notebook. Banque Lambert is illegal in the Congo so I have to be on the alert.

A HUB OF OPPORTUNITIES AND OPPORTUNISM

'The misery of some makes for the happiness of others' – an adage that proved to be true for Mathilde in the aftermath of the Nyiragongo eruption of January 2002 which destroyed between 15 per cent and 20 per cent of the city's buildings and infrastructure. Mathilde's affairs took a turn for the better. On the recommendation of her lover at the time – a hardware and building material wholesaler – she followed in his footsteps and got involved in the same business. After the eruption, demand skyrocketed, piggybacking on the already strong demand from urban expansion. The market, in the words of her lover, was 'juicy'. He took her on a few buying excursions to Kampala, Nairobi and Dar es Salaam to buy cement, metal rods, tiles, glass windows, electric supplies, plumbing equipment, metal roofing and all kinds of smaller hardware items such as nails and screws and tools. She caught on fast with his coaching.

'I was amazed by the way I could turn over a profit. Selling this stuff was a real bonanza. My bar and wholesale alcohol activities were doing well and, with the staff I hired to run them, continued to bring in money. It was a great place to have my own business meetings with hardware buyers.' This period constituted the height of her prosperity. She sent her son to study architecture in Kinshasa, was a fashion figurehead in the neighbourhood and welcomed four needy family members to live with her – looked after by a full-time servant. Getting from one meeting to another became easy when one of her clients who did not have the cash to repay his debts gave her his Toyota Carina in lieu of cash. Another deal presented itself shortly afterwards and she acquired a Mitsubishi Pajero jeep. 'Money kept on coming in so I bought a little house made of wooden planks in the Ndosho area to rent out. The rent wasn't much but proved the logic that says water runs into the river. It was in this context of dizzying success that I fell … rock bottom.'

'Life isn't always beautiful in the world of mortals,' philosophises Mathilde with a melancholy sigh. 'I've had so many ups and downs and twists and turns. When I thought I was riding high, destiny had another idea. My fall was a shock.' She fell sick in 2010 and was hospitalised again. 'That was a real tragedy. I didn't have anyone to help me with my activities and the competition was intense.' Her earnings could not cover her hospital bills so she used her savings. The hardware business and the wholesale alcohol depot were shut down because the workers were not able to manage them adequately – 'They had neither my professional savvy nor my public relations talent. Luckily the bar kept afloat.' She had to sell the Toyota, and, shortly afterwards, her brother-in-law wrecked the Pajero in an accident.

Fearful of spending all her money at hospital in Goma, she swallowed her pride and asked her older brother, who was living in Kinshasa, for help. He paid for her airfare and care at the University of Kinshasa clinic. After a series of operations, which were spread out over a six-month period, she recovered but stayed another two months to rest. 'All this cost my brother the astronomical amount of $6,000!' It did not take long after landing in Goma for her to see what had happened to the bar that had taken her so much energy to develop. 'It was a mess! I was lucky to be able to salvage a few plastic chairs and tables that I brought home to start over again by selling soft drinks. Once again, I found myself at square one.'

Between debacles and disillusionment – in addition to the physical energy needed to pick up the pieces – she fell ill again with serious back problems. This time she stayed three months in the Goma hospital for the physically handicapped. Fragile but still on the alert for business opportunities, she mustered her remaining savings and gave them to her sister's husband to buy mobile phones in Dubai. With the help of a friend in Kinshasa, she sold them on credit. This – plus the sale of a portion of her land – led her to initiate her own trips to Dubai where she bought laptop computers to sell in Goma. The latest avatar of her professional reincarnation is employment in the provincial administration: 'You never know what an administrative job can lead to in this town.' Mathilde complains that her life 'hasn't been a bed of roses' but she is determined to 'rise again like the proverbial phoenix. I have to – for my children and for the love of God.' Mathilde's story is one of self-reliance and resilience. 'Never give up. Fight and fight more. I'm not frightened by the future because I know I have the smile and the determination to make life move in the direction I want it to.'

CHAPTER 2

THE AMAZING
WOODEN SCOOTER

THE TSHUKUDU

The *tshukudu* (pronounced tchou-kou-dou) is an emblematic symbol of the city of Goma. A large wooden contraption that looks like a hybrid between a scooter and a bicycle, its wheels rimmed with strips of recycled lorry tyres, it is a workable solution to Goma's transportation needs. It looks odd but commands respect. The product of the creative and pragmatic spirit of the people of the region, this amazing two-wheeled invention seems anachronistic. Notwithstanding its charm, it is incongruous in a twenty-first-century cityscape. Its designers could have named it something like 'wooden bike' or 'wooden scooter' but chose instead the onomatopoetic *tshu-ku-du*, *tshu-ku-du*, *tshu-ku-du*, reproducing the sound it makes as it scurries along Goma's lava-stone streets.

The shape of its handlebars, which look like they were inspired by the short and slender horns of Kivu cattle, reinforces its odd appearance. 'That is a perfectly appropriate coincidence because the *tshukudu* could be considered as some sort of mythical beast of burden. It moves down our hills heavily laden with produce but climbs back up thanks to the strong biceps of its driver,' says Cerezo, the protagonist of this narrative. Most farmers from the Goma hinterland have adopted the *tshukudu* to transport their goods to Goma's marketplaces because it can be used in situations where other kinds of vehicles would not serve as well. 'Someone else invented the wheel, we perfected it with the *tshukudu*.' The *tshukudeur* (the driver) moves throughout the city from dawn to nightfall carrying the most surprising loads.

The invention is a unique and inimitable symbol for the population of Goma, who have wholeheartedly embraced its significance. The municipality erected a giant statue of a *tshukudu* and *tshukudeur*, which towers over one of the city's busiest intersections. The official name of the intersection is Bralima, but everyone just refers to it as the '*Tshukudu* roundabout'. It is the place par excellence where anyone wishing to immortalise a visit to the city must be photographed. Even in the days of the selfie, photographers still linger there harassing potential customers to take their portrait. There are other important roundabouts in Goma, such as *Signers* with its Nyiragongo monument surrounded by sculptures of mountain gorillas, and BDGL by the picturesque colonial post office – which the people of Goma vainly like to think of as being Congo's largest roundabout – but none of these other places can compete with the prestige of the *Tshukudu* roundabout.

The craftsmen who make *tshukudus* consider themselves artists and pretend to be the inventors. Simpler versions, however, were used by children elsewhere in the Kivus as playthings. 'It's true that kids used them as scooters to race down the steep hills of the region, but the version we use in Goma today is a real *Gomatracien* invention for utilitarian purposes. This funny-looking two-wheeler testifies to our Congolese creative talents.'

Cerezo belongs to Goma's *tshukudeur* informal brotherhood, which he emphasises is 'a man's world'. He is a big strong man with a beard who navigates his *tshukudu* with the help of his adolescent nephew Kiditcho. When you see them together you feel an instinctive complementarity. 'I don't have to tell the kid what to do. He is a careful observer who can adapt to problem situations by making the right moves. He is a big help to me on these roads full of unexpected obstacles, where, in the wink of an eye, you can find yourself bruised and bloody on the ground with your stuff all over the place.'

The presence of this 'poor man's motorbike' among the host of local transportation options responds to the particular challenges of the urban and peri-urban social and physical environments. There are swarms of young men who have to fend for themselves with the 'might of their muscles and the power of their determination'. Poor road conditions within the city and in the outskirts limit automobile traffic, which also explains the omnipresence of the *tshukudu*. 'My comrades and I are ready to transport agricultural produce from outlying villages to the city, carry heavy construction material from hardware stores to the newly mushrooming neighbourhoods, and move whatever else people may ask us. For short and long distances, my wheelbarrow-bicycle-scooter combi can do it.'

CEREZO'S PAST AND PRESENT

Cerezo comes from a *tshukudu* family. He has been surrounded by them since childhood: his father makes them and his brothers either make or drive them. The family is from Kibumba, a village well known for its important produce market 30 kilometres north of Goma. The spectacle of a *tshukudu* overloaded with bags of vegetables coasting down the road towards the city is an everyday occurrence.

Jacob, my father, was a pioneer when it comes to using the *tshukudu* for transportation between Kibumba and Goma. At the time, *tshukudus* were even more rudimentary than now; the different components didn't fit that well together which made transporting heavy loads impractical. These difficulties inspired Papa Jacob to convert into a *tshukudu* maker and set up a workshop. He improved the use of the design by raising the frame, adding recycled springs as shock absorbers on the front wheel and adding ball bearings in metal hubs in both wheels. That's why *tshukudus* today can carry loads that weigh 300 kilos.

The updated 'rustic and robust machine that rolls smoothly' requires little maintenance. 'All we need is some used motor oil for the ball bearings, a protective oil for the wood, which takes a beating from the near daily showers and humidity, and a few nails to keep the rubber tyres attached to the wooden wheels – plus our ties to keep our loads attached, cut from old inner tubes or tyres.'

In their seventies, Cerezo's parents are still active. 'My mother still farms for the family's table and sells what's left over. Papa is as busy as ever making and repairing *tshukudus* in his workshop.' All the boys followed in the footsteps of their father to earn their living, and his sisters – who are all married – took after their mother, tilling the land and growing crops. None of the siblings spent much time in school because their parents were unable to scrape together the money needed for fees. 'We survived thanks to mother's hard work in her fields. We learned quickly that we had no business asking how much Papa earned and even less what he did with his money. But it wasn't hard to figure out. He would stagger back home late, smelling of alcohol. That made me vow never to drink and – latter on – to join a Protestant church.'

Cerezo spent his boyhood either in the fields with Caroline, his mother, helping her tend to her cabbages, leeks, onions and potatoes, or in his father's workshop, observing him at work and helping by handing him a hammer, nails or a machete. Exposure to both these worlds provided him with the background he needed to be a good *tshukudeur*: he learned to distinguish between good and poor produce and how to transport it. 'Unlike my brothers, who copied my father is his drinking habits and refusal to pick up a hoe, I think that farming is important and I do what I can to improve my harvests.' His affinity for farming came gradually, encouraged by his mother, who gave him bits of land that he could cultivate to earn his own money. 'I became good at farming thanks to my mother and I'm grateful for that.'

> I cobbled together my own little *tshukudu* as a kid and used it to speed down the path that led to the river where we would bathe. I had plenty of mishaps with it and one time I sprained my wrist. Papa comforted my sobs with a vigorous massage, telling me, 'You have to learn to put up with pain; that's how you grow up to be a real man.'

When he got bigger, Cerezo accompanied his older brothers to Goma, helping them with their vegetable-laden *tshukudus*. It took some time but he gradually learned the ropes.

> I mastered the tricks of the trade pretty much automatically. It wasn't a deliberate decision – becoming a *tshukudeur* was something that just came naturally. I never asked anyone if I could become a *tshukudeur* and no one asked me to become one. I have no regrets about the way it turned out because it's an occupation that allows me to fend for my family.
>
> Destiny has turned me into both *tshukudeur* and farmer and a bit of a tinker in the workshop. I'm not bad when it comes to making *tshukudus* but prefer not spending too much time with my father and brothers who harass me to go out drinking with them or beg me

for beer money. If they really need money for something else, however, I'm willing to help out.

Cerezo gives the impression of being someone who tries to avoid conflict, both in his family and with his fellow *tshukudeurs*. 'If a colleague in distress needs some help along the road, I'll lend a hand. But if I have the feeling that I'm being taken advantage of, I'll keep my distance.' These situations are infrequent, so they do not discourage Cerezo from considering that his life as a *tshukudeur* – his life since age seventeen – is good. Luck, *'la providence'*, he believes, matters. One Sunday after church services, a friend, Dieudonné, invited him to meet an acquaintance, a hotel manager, who was looking for a vegetable supplier for the restaurant.

> Thanks to the Hotel Ishango manager, Mr Mawazo, I joined the circle of hotel suppliers. Dieudonné introduced me as a reliable *tshukudeur* with a good supply backup network. Mr Mawazo and I hit it off immediately. I had the impression that he was kind and generous and felt that he sensed that I was honest. Even though we were not from the same region or ethnic group, he took to me. On the first Tuesday that we met, he placed an order for a large quantity of various vegetables for the following Friday.

The manager said he was pleased with the first delivery when he saw it and made arrangements for regular deliveries. He paid $40 on the spot without any bargaining.

I had the feeling that I was taking advantage of the man. It was the first time in my life that I ever had so much money in my pocket – my own money! Perceiving that I felt guilty, he asked: 'The hotel is paying for this you know – and do you have any idea of the profit we are going to make with your cabbage and celery?' I regained my composure, understanding that this Mr Mawazo was a benediction for me.

A snag became apparent immediately: Cerezo was not able to read the list of items on his order sheet. 'I was lost trying to figure out words like rhubarb and celery but luckily Dieudonné came to the rescue.' Cerezo then decided to take private reading and arithmetic lessons with a cousin by the name of Leopold, who was a teacher. 'At twenty I came to grasp the importance of these basic skills for self-reliance – for me and everyone else.' With Leopold's help, Cerezo was soon able to manage on his own.

Cerezo likes to repeat the adage 'he who finds a wife finds happiness'. He did indeed find one, which he considers another stroke of good fortune.

It was my mother who pointed out Fanny to me, an eighteen-year-old girl from the neighbourhood in Kibumba. I didn't feel ready to assume new responsibilities and wasn't even particularly attracted to her. Although I was earning more cash than my brothers who were already married, I wasn't interested in girls. I had some vague plans for the future about what to do with my money but marriage wasn't one of them. But my mother was stubborn about Fanny and insisted that she was a good little farm girl who could grow plenty of vegetables for me to sell. She also sang the praises of her sisters who had all given birth to healthy babies. I ended up by agreeing.

As Caroline already had the consent of Fanny's family, the only remaining obstacle was Cerezo's father. Not only did Papa Jacob approve, he readily agreed to pay for Cerezo's dowry – two cows – just as he had done for his other sons. The engagement ceremony took place as soon as Jacob accepted. Jacob's support was a surprise to Cerezo, who admitted that he had judged his father's drinking habits too harshly. 'I had enough money stashed away to pay for a wedding worthy of an independent, self-reliant *tshuku-deur* like myself and to put up a little house in the family compound to welcome my new bride. At twenty-two, I was married and the following year we were the proud parents of a beautiful little girl we named Caroline, after my mother.'

Other children followed, a responsibility Cerezo takes seriously: 'I preside over the destinies of six souls – four kids', Fanny's and my own.' Caroline's predictions did not fall far from the mark. 'Fanny has turned out to be hard-working and productive in the fields, contributing to the family's progress. I do not regret listening to my mother's entreaties. Fanny helped me discover the meaning of love.' Her contribution also allowed them to roof their house with iron sheeting – a sign of prestige in the area. Their two oldest children attend school: 'I was deprived of that opportunity but am determined that my children are not. I want them to have a better life than mine.'

Cerezo works part time as a *tshukudeur*, depending on market days. Twice a week (Tuesdays and Fridays) he goes to Goma to deliver vegetables to Mr Mawazo and other hotel restaurants. Monday, with Fanny's help, is devoted to gathering the items for the orders. If his own or his mother's fields do not have the necessary items, he buys directly from neighbours, people he has known since childhood and who let him pay after collecting his money in town. 'Fanny does the bargaining. She is much better at it than me. We prefer buying from them opposed to the local market where we would have to pay higher prices in cash on the spot.'

Cerezo and Kiditcho, his faithful assistant, are ready at 5 am on market days with the merchandise carefully tied down on his *tshukudu*. As the road from Kibumba to Goma is a gradual descent, his loads can average up to 300 kilos. 'We can coast down all the way to town. When traffic gets congested, that's when I really need Kiditcho.' Once the deliveries are made and orders for the next trip are taken, they tarry in town just long enough to pay a few social calls or to go to Birere, where Cerezo picks up a few things for Fanny: salt, oil, soap and other such items. Cerezo does not feel comfortable in the city, which he finds noisy, over-crowded and full of pickpockets. He also feels threatened by the greedy looks of the police, 'who are very interested in what's in my pocket'. It is a relief for him to get back home to Kibumba with no mishaps. Kiditcho gets his cut before leaving Goma so that he can rummage through piles of used clothing, hoping to replace his worn-out old trainers or find a pair of jeans or a polo shirt.

> More often than not, however, the boy asks me to hold on to his money for a rainy day. It shows that he has some sense, which augurs well for his future. I was the same way when I was his age. Maybe that's why I have a paternal feeling of affection for Kiditcho. He lives under my roof and Fanny feeds him but I still give him a wage; the equivalent of a fifth of my earnings, which average between $25 and $35 a week. The relationship I have with Kiditcho is fairly common in our circle of *tshukudeurs*; we consider our helpers as apprentices and they consider us as masters.

They head back to the village the same day in the afternoon and usually can get a lift for themselves and their *tshukudu* with one of the many lorries that travel the same road. Fully loaded when going to Goma from the food-producing northern region of North Kivu or from Uganda, the lorries are usually empty when leaving Goma. 'The drivers ask for a few dollars but sometimes they take us for free.' As soon as he gets back, Cerezo settles his debts with his mother and the other farmers for their vegetables.

Cerezo, a sober and taciturn man, also takes his farm work seriously. He clears and tills his plots with the help of day labourers. Fanny takes over with the planting, weeding, trimming and harvesting – also with some paid outside help. Over the years, they have been able to steadily increase the number of their plots, which allows them to satisfy most of their clients' needs while also earning the reputation of being reliable suppliers.

> Even though I didn't wear out my pants on a school bench, I made up for it with lessons as a young man. My abilities are sketchy, but enough not to be taken advantage of by dodgy hotel managers and restaurant owners. Some of my *tshukudeur* colleagues make fun of my broken French and crazy spelling but I don't care. I earn more money than them and their French doesn't help them manoeuvre a *tshukudu*.

Between farming and shuttling between Kibumba and Goma with his *tshukudu*, Cerezo does not have much spare time. 'All this work keeps me out of trouble. Anyway, I don't have the money to waste on trifles.' Sunday, he goes to church and spends time with the family, his only down time. He has been a practising Protestant since his teenage years and claims to have found spiritual well-being. Fanny shares his convictions, claiming: 'God protects me, blesses my home and has given me steady work. That's why I struggle to respect his commandments – like being humble and respecting the Sabbath. My days, weeks and months roll on and all look the same but I have no complaints. I don't ask myself too many questions.'

THE TSHUKUDEUR
BROTHERHOOD

Cerezo knows most of the approximately fifty *tshukudeurs* who live in Kibumba. 'If one of us has a problem, the others lend a hand. Solidarity between us is spontaneous. The urban *tshukudeurs* based in Goma have an association but I don't think that offers any advantage. Our way of doing things is more flexible and efficient.' Sometimes solidarity can take the form of moral support, such as helping a colleague gather up produce that has scattered if the driver has lost control, or vociferously getting involved in an argument between a *tshukudeur* and a police officer – which attracts the interest of passers-by, putting the officer in a bad light. 'This kind of problem, however, doesn't happen very often,' he admits. Mutual support is forthcoming in cases of 'happy and unhappy events of life' such as buying gifts for newborns and contributing to funeral costs. 'Some of my colleagues can be tight-fisted but I play the role of mediator, explaining that a tragedy can strike any one of us so relieving someone's suffering even a little is a good thing.'

The question of formal or informal organisation is unimportant to Cerezo, who just feels good in the company of his kindred *tshukudeurs*. Even when they have different destinations in the morning, they like to congregate to leave Kibumba together before going their own separate ways.

I wait for the others to be ready to start the descent. Everyone knows that departure is at 5 am and gets organised to not make the others wait. Travelling by group has saved us on more than one occasion. A lone *tshukudeur* is more vulnerable to crazy men with guns than a group. In past periods of really bad insecurity, MONUSCO escorted us with their armoured vehicles and even once by helicopter.

Each *tshukudeur* is accompanied by at least one or two helpers whose job is to help keep balance and push while the 'master' steers the handlebar. 'It's not easy with our heavy loads and bumpy roads. I won't dare tell you how often I fall. When it happens, it requires incredible strength to get the *tshukudu* standing again.'

Shuttling between Kibumba and Goma with produce is one thing, but the *tshukudeurs* who work solely in the Goma streets need other talents. 'First, they have to learn the rules of the road to avoid problems with police and accidents with pedestrians, cars, lorries, bicycles, motorbikes, handcarts and other *tshukudeurs*.' Adapting to these demands is reflected in street protocol: 'We village *tshukudeurs* tend to be calm and reserved. Our city colleagues on the other hand are rude, abrupt, noisy and stubborn as they thread through traffic.' Cerezo says that he would not be able to cope with the intense city work on a daily basis because of the congestion and the nature of the loads, such as corrugated iron roofing, planks, bags of cement, wooden beams made of eucalyptus tree trunks and similar construction materials needed to serve the thriving house construction sector. Market traders expect *tshukudeurs* to transport bags full of beans, potatoes and bundles of other produce, *makala*, even sides of beef from the slaughterhouse. 'I can manage bundles of cabbage and carrots but don't ask me to transport four easy chairs at once, which is something my urban colleagues can do.'

THE UGLY DUCKING

Like other African cities, Goma's streets are packed with minibuses, pickups, lorries, motorbikes, bicycles, cars and SUVs (usually with the logo of an NGO painted on the door). With its improbable loads, the *tshukudu* has its place among these other vehicles. Concentrating on the stability of his load, the *tshukudeur* navigates through the traffic with the sole objective of getting his goods to their destination. Similarly, the other drivers do not seem to be bothered by them. 'Goma is like that; its population accepts different social realities and allows all kinds of livelihood strategies to co-exist.' The question of how something like the *tshukudu* can survive in the twenty-first century in a city that has willingly embraced different forms of modernity does not disturb Cerezo: 'Just like an ugly duckling surrounded by swans, the *tshukudeur* goes about his business headstrong, in this city where the bizarre has become commonplace.'

Cerezo is not dissatisfied with his double life as farmer and *tshukudeur*. 'I earn a decent living and feel pretty well off.' But there is a hint of self-doubt and contradiction in his discourse. 'I'm not about to let my sons follow in my footsteps like Papa Jacob did with my brothers and me. I'm paying for my kids to go to school so they can have a better life than me. To avoid my destiny of hard toil, I'm helping them study as long as possible.' His ambition is that his offspring live in the city and have diplomas. He also tries to deposit $20 a week in a savings account to buy a house lot in Goma.

> Land prices in the north of the Virunga neighbourhood are still reasonable, and, from what I've been told, I should be able to pay in instalments. My kids have to get out of the village so they can wash with water that flows from a tap and see at night by flicking on a switch. That is the best way they'll be able to care for me when I'm too old to work.

Even though Cerezo does not want his sons to be *tshukudeurs*, he believes that – for purely pragmatic reasons – the unique wooden scooter is going to be needed by the Goma population for years to come. 'The social and economic situation of Goma is not going to improve over night so there will be plenty of strong young men without real jobs struggling to survive. Goma is still a city that relies on muscle so becoming a *tshukudeur* is an option for them.' Cerezo sees himself as a kind of bridge connecting city and village, and that a dynamic symbiotic relationship thrives thanks to the interactions between 'the good and the bad, rich and poor and modern and backwards'. Among them, the *tshukudeur* has his place. He feeds the population and helps build the city by carrying construction materials into the expanding outer sections. 'We may look funny on our amazing wooden invention but we are not ashamed. No one should look down on us. We are part of the city and *Gomatraciens* just as much as anyone else.'

CHAPTER 3

CHARCOAL IS LIFE

LIBOKO THE CHARCOAL MAN

Nguba Liboko was born on the island of Idjwi in Lake Kivu in October 1969. He lived there for the first fifteen years of his life with his family, and, like many other children of his age, he went to school, fished, helped his parents farm and got into mischief. 'My parents were primarily farmers and produced charcoal from the trees cut down to clear their plots. Making charcoal isn't complicated if you know what you are doing and I caught on just by watching.' They did not, however, sell their *makala* (the Swahili and Lingala word for charcoal) or even use it themselves. Liboko's mother cooked with wood between three stones – which is the technique still used in many parts of rural DRC. On Idjwi at that time women had not started using *mbabula* (charcoal cooking stoves made of scrap metal) because wood was still abundant. They would give away their *makala* to friends stopping off on the island from the boats plying the lake between Bukavu and Goma – because *mbabula* were starting to be common on the urban landscape.

A cholera epidemic ravaged the island's population in 1981, leaving many dead – including Liboko's mother and father. 'I was miraculously spared but found myself alone at twelve years old. I had to drop out of my last year of primary school because no one was around to pay my fees. Neighbours who took over the family land helped me a little in the beginning but only half-heartedly.' The young boy quickly learned to fend for himself.

'Liboko' was a childhood nickname. It literally means 'strong arm', which suited the boy well because he loved paddling his dugout canoe and consequently developed large biceps. The boy definitively adopted his nickname when he left school. As Liboko was an excellent swimmer and paddler he was eager to help people in difficulty in the water – people whose dugout canoes capsized, for example. 'Everyone around the Ruhundu port knew me and my skills. The lake was my playground.' Paradoxically, his reputation was the reason why he left the island. In 1984 he was hired by the Société Nationale des Chemins de fer du Zaïre (SNCZ) – which managed the Bukavu port – as the resident lifeguard.

At fifteen, Liboko was a clueless young man with a strong body and a steady salary. Never having received any advice on how to manage money, he squandered it. 'I had no idea of the value of cash and used to say *franka ina ni kifu* [money is a nuisance].' He would spend his evenings in bars, drinking and buying beer for strangers who became little more than fair-weather friends. But during the day he had to work and train. 'My body turned into steel and I looked like an athlete. You can imagine how the girls used to hover about – like bees around honey.'

Wrinkled and worn by a hard life today, his self-proclaimed sex appeal of yesteryear, however, got him into deep trouble: 'I didn't have the willpower or the common sense to avoid my boss's wife.' They had an affair, his boss found out, and Liboko had to run for his life. His work at the Bukavu port had lasted three years.

> I was inexperienced with women and naïve about life in general. My boss's wife was beautiful and much older than I was. I didn't get what she saw in me. She was irresistible with a perfume that swept me away. She bought me nice clothes and coached me in the ways of the world. The vanity and adrenaline of it all went to my head. Having forgotten that I was still a boy, I thought she had turned me into a man. My promising future vanished overnight because of my stupidity. If I had the chance to start over again, I'd certainly do things differently.

He knew that he would never be able to find work as a lifeguard on Lake Kivu again. 'Hunted like a wild animal by my boss's men and just barely escaping with my life, I had to start over from scratch.' One of his drinking mates dissuaded him from returning to Idjwi, which was his first reaction, arguing that he would be looked for there. Taking that as sound advice, Liboko sought refuge in Kalehe, a village on the Bukavu–Goma road. Chance would have it that he ran into friends of his parents who were willing to take him in. The main subsistence and commercial activity in Kalehe was farming, but Liboko was not inclined to pick up the hoe and machete he left on his parents' land. Producing charcoal – which he still remembered how to do – seemed a better option at the time. 'The work demanded physical energy and tenacity. I had the first and strove to develop the other.' He did indeed apply himself but earned little, mainly because the roads to both Bukavu and Goma were winding with unsafe climbs and descents. There were therefore lots of accidents, which pushed up transportation costs. After four years of effort, he had to face facts: 'I needed to try my luck elsewhere; I wasn't going to get ahead in Kalehe.' Still haunted by the lingering fear of returning to Bukavu, he decided to head for the Goma area. Liboko gives the impression of having learned more from his mistakes than from his achievements.

In 1991, Liboko moved to Sake. 'Sake was a busy little town with lots of trade with Goma just nearby. There would be new challenges but it seemed that the *makala* business would work there.' The main difference between rural Kalehe and urbanised Sake in terms of the *makala* trade is wood supply. In Kalehe, Liboko got wood for free from the family with whom he lived. They were happy to give it to him because he did the hard work of cutting down the trees and clearing the land they would farm. Access to trees around Sake was difficult because the only forests in the area were within the Virunga National Park. The other forested areas belonged to people who knew their worth and even planted trees. 'I didn't have a choice;

I was going to have to buy trees. But the dynamism of the Sake marketplace, compared to the free wood of Kalehe, made it worth the gamble.'

It did not take long for Liboko to realise that working solo had its limits. 'I lost opportunities to make money because I couldn't keep up with demand.' Having gradually become familiar with the local business dynamics and people, Liboko went into partnership with a few acquaintances. They were men who had experience working within the park and knew how to corrupt park rangers from the Congolese Institute for Nature Conservation (ICCN). 'They would turn a blind eye to what we all knew was an illegal activity – producing charcoal inside the park.' Operating inside the park with accomplices allowed him to double the earnings he made when he worked alone. 'In Kalehe I didn't have to deal with police officers, soldiers or environmental agents. In Sake it was different but I was able to work things out once I learned to respect the game of the nod and the wink.'

Their team comprised three 'chiefs' and three 'apprentices' who would work together, participating in the physical labour and in sharing the profits. 'We could produce up to 200 60 kilo bags a month.' When the load was ready, they would call for a lorry to pick it up and deliver it to a depot in Goma. They had to depend on a depot owner who rented them space; the owner reserved the right to sell their charcoal himself. Liboko would remain idle until the load was sold by this intermediary. Depot owners in Goma work with multiple suppliers at the same time so Liboko would usually have to wait between three days and a week before the load was sold and he could collect his earnings: the sale price of the charcoal minus the rental fees charged by the depot owner. Liboko would then head back to the park, find his partners and start the cycle over again.

Things seemed to be going smoothly for Liboko but ill fortune struck again. Scrambling to get away from a falling tree, he tripped and broke his arm. 'I miscalculated the direction of the fall. It was just bad luck.' His comrades took him to Goma to hospital where his arm was put in a plaster cast. There was nevertheless an upside to the accident because his convalescence gave him the opportunity to make new plans. 'I had plenty of time to ponder while waiting for my arm to heal. That was when I thought about, and figured out the costs of, renting our own depot.' His job in the team of dealing with relations with depot owners allowed him to observe how that relatively lucrative link in the *makala* value chain was run.

With the support of his colleagues, he began the search for a depot, which he found near the Ndosho market, just a few metres off the road to Sake.

It was a small room three metres by four and cost us two bags of charcoal per month. I slept in it too, amongst the bags of *makala*. As I couldn't help my comrades in the forest because of my arm, I had to do something to help because they were covering my doctor's bills and living expenses. There was a strong sense of solidarity between us. In the beginning, it was a temporary plan until my arm healed and I could get back to the forest, but somehow I had the feeling that life was taking on a new direction without really knowing where I was headed.

Liboko was helping the team by selling their *makala* in Goma much more than participating in its actual production. Seeing their increase in profits, they asked him to stick with it – while they would pursue the production without him. 'Although I never admitted it to the others, I was relieved by the new arrangement. Ever since my problems in Bukavu, I had become wary – and carrying out illegal incursions into the Virunga Park gave me nightmares. I didn't like taking those kinds of risks.' ICCN does in fact have a designated – albeit relatively powerless – anti-charcoal brigade.

In 1995, the *makala* production business was seriously disrupted throughout the Goma hinterland. In the wake of the Rwandan genocide 'refugees invaded the park, cornering the *makala* business, pushing prices down. No one could stop them.' Liboko and his comrades could not compete and their profits dwindled. Their partnership dissolved, and, after settling their accounts, they all went their separate ways. Some of his ex-partners owned land and took up farming – or returned to it. Agriculture was a highly profitable business in those days because the international NGOs who flocked to the region to assist the refugees 'paid good money for food'. Without land of his own, and disinclined to farm for others, Liboko kept the depot and started selling charcoal for other producers. 'I wasn't bringing in as much money as before but, as I didn't have to share with anyone, I was able to make ends meet.'

Shortly after the partnership broke up, Liboko left the relatively poor Ndosho neighbourhood to set up shop in the busier commercial area of Majengo, next to two other charcoal sellers. 'There were also food wholesalers on my new street, a petrol station and lots of small shops selling this and that.' Charcoal retailers who sold little plastic bags of charcoal along the street or in a nearby secondary market were his biggest customers. 'They would buy full bags at a time. In those days a bag of *makala* was worth $20.[1] When business was good, I could sell up to 600 bags a month.'

THE GAUNTLET FROM FOREST TO MARKET

Liboko went into the *makala* business mainly because he didn't have any other options. The fact that he had some idea of how to produce it from his childhood days on Idjwi was a contributing factor.

I haven't had it easy. My parents died before I could think straight and I didn't have the luck to stay in school. Complaining isn't going to change things but I just can't help thinking about my early misfortune. I don't have a lot of options so do the best I can to make ends meet thanks to *makala*. I do whatever I can to turn over a profit even though it is a risky business. Getting my *makala* to Goma from the park can be life-threatening in this environment where you just don't know what can happen.

Liboko has been involved in the three main steps of the charcoal supply chain: producing it in the forest, transporting it from the forest to the market, and wholesale trade. He had to deal with a complicated set of actors at each step. Selling *makala* in Goma is not dangerous or particularly challenging from an administrative or commercial perspective – 'you just have to pay off the right people' – but production and transportation are 'activities fraught with danger and full of surprises because the Goma hinterland is a security nightmare. Anyone can sell in town but work in the forest is another story.'

The initial phase starts with finding trees that are known to produce charcoal that ignites easily and simmers for a long time – two important criteria for a cook. The trees should be in an accessible area and be just the right size: if they are too big or too small they don't burn properly in the oven. They have to be chopped down, cut into pieces, stacked and then blanketed with earth. This pile of earth-covered wood (called an oven or a kiln) is then ignited and monitored carefully. The smouldering process can take up to a couple of weeks. Once the fire has died down and the charcoal has cooled off, it is bagged and then carried and stored in a nearby village until a lorry can come to pick it up. An operation like this can last up to two months.

Liboko has to do whatever he can to maintain his supply of *makala*. Sometimes when he goes into the forest, it is to buy from villagers who produce it for sale; at other times he goes to organise his own production. 'I prefer producing my own *makala* because I can control the quality and manage my time more efficiently. It may not seem like much but my experience counts for something.' It is a competitive business because it attracts lots of young men with limited skills or work opportunities.

> But it isn't easy to succeed at it, because in addition to some technical *savoir faire*, you need to know how to behave with village folk. If the village chief or the owner of a forest doesn't like you, you're in trouble. They are the ones who dictate the prices without needing to negotiate. The demand is so high that it is a seller's market, where the buyer just has to say amen. Some village chiefs require a fee just so you can look at trees inside their forests. If the forest is interesting, you pay a fixed amount of money to cut as many trees as you want within a carefully defined area. Other chiefs want you to pay a certain sum per tree depending on its size and species.

As scouting out suitable forest areas is a big part of the work, Liboko has established a network of intermediaries whom he pays in beer for information. 'If I get some good deals from them, however, I show my gratitude by giving them money or *makala* when I get back to town.' He also has a similar arrangement with intermediaries in the different villages where he has worked who help him find bags of charcoal or chiefs willing to sell trees.

Once he has a sufficiently large load of bagged charcoal, the second step starts – getting it from the village to Goma. Liboko considers it the riskiest and most dangerous part of the operation. As he does not have his own lorry, he is dependent on the whims and availability of professional transporters. It is impossible to calculate with any certainty when the load will be constituted (that depends on local villagers who help him carry it), which means that he cannot arrange for a lorry to come for it in advance. If the village is near a road, he can call for a lorry, but if it is more isolated, he has to leave his precious *makala* and go and negotiate with a driver and then show him the way. There is risk and stress involved in leaving the load, as it can be stolen.

It is a cut-throat environment where only the clever survive. Once I'm lucky enough to have my *makala* loaded onto a lorry, I have to start worrying about other traps along the road. With even the best driver, I still pay something at each road block. We have learned to keep a very low profile to avoid attracting attention. Those soldiers, rebels and other men with guns can be unpredictable and trigger-happy. What are you going to do if they want to search you or take your belongings? If you resist, or even if you throw an insolent glance, you'll find yourself with a bullet in the gut or decapitated with a blow from a machete.

Despite these very real security risks, people continue to move about. To minimise such risks, however, lorry drivers are forced to make long detours that push up travel fees. For Liboko, the additional fees are just one more sacrifice to make to stay in business by avoiding supply shortages. 'I don't have the choice if I want to keep my customers coming back.' It is uncommon for Liboko to transport a load of charcoal without some kind of adventure, which is why he admits: 'When I reach Goma alive and with my cargo intact, I give a sigh of relief.' The transporter does too, who receives 20 per cent of Liboko's earnings after the load has been sold.

On two separate occasions, Liboko thought that he was about to see his last days on earth. 'In 2009, I was taken hostage for two months by a group of Mai-Mai fighters near Kanyabayonga, 200 kilometres north of Goma where I had some *makala* ovens going. I was lucky and they let me go. My experience near Kiwandja in 2011 was much worse. I was threatened by M23 rebels who took everything I had.' Like other people who overcome trauma, Liboko gives thanks to God after surviving these narrow escapes. 'When I get back to my friends and family safe and sound from the forest I praise the Lord. Even when I lost everything I had, I knew that my prayers reached God's ear. As long as I still have my arms and legs and my

head, I'll keep up the struggle for survival with his benediction.' The defeat of the M23 rebellion in November 2013
was a source of optimism for the population of Goma,
who hope that the other groups that terrorise the region
will also be crushed. 'To work, everyone needs security,
especially us in the *makala* business.'

NO MAKALA, NO DINNER

Few homes in Goma are connected to the electric grid
because the sector is neglected by the state and under-
developed. Even fewer homes have electric stoves, and
those that do cannot depend on them alone for cooking
because of the frequent power cuts that can last days
at a time. Only well-off families can afford to run their
petrol-powered generators to cook. Despite the negative
environmental consequences, charcoal is the logical alternative. 'Just about everyone in Goma – rich and poor – relies
on *makala* to prepare their daily dishes of beans,' declares
an emphatic Liboko. But access to this vital commodity
is difficult because there are few available forested areas
around the city, which is hemmed in between the Virunga
Park and Lake Kivu. The thorny bushes that grow in
the black lava gravel of Goma, according to Liboko, 'are
useless because they burn without giving any embers'.

A few woody areas do exist, such as the Tumaini school
concession or the old archdiocese, both of which belong to
the Catholic Church. But they are off limits, as are the few
remaining trees along Goma's avenues, a vestige of the
colonial period. The municipality does not have a tree-

planting policy and individuals who wish to plant fruit or decorative trees on their lots have to first break through the ground with metal tools, dig, bring in planting soil, buy the tree and then plant it. 'It's a big investment to have some shade or a few pieces of fruit. Moreover, there are practically no nurseries in Goma, which proves how small a priority tree planting is in Goma.' Another problem relates to ownership rights: renters are not automatically allowed to plant trees on land belonging to their owners. Liboko specifies that there are also administrative concerns.

> When someone succeeds in planting a tree in his garden, he can't do what he wants with it. Environmental agents see the tree as an opportunity for harassment. If you want to cut it down, you need to pay for authorisation. If you cut it down anyway, you'll get fined. 'It's your tree as long as you struggle to make it grow. When it is strong and healthy, it becomes state property' is something I've heard environment agents say.

Cooking with *makala* is driven by culture just as much as it is by availability and cost considerations. Many people believe that getting the right taste of certain foods – such as *sombe* (cassava leaves) and some fish and meat preparations – can only be achieved thanks to the smoky smell of *makala*. Cooking with wood can also give those tastes, but it has largely disappeared from city life, due in part to pollution from smoke and soot. 'Only the most indigent people of Goma cook with wood scavenged from here and there, even though they know that it is a public announcement of their poverty. A whole neighbourhood can become infested with the smoke from a single wood fire.'

The donor community and international environmental NGOs have been active in trying to come up with solutions to help people while reducing pressure on the Virunga National Park at the same time. There are a few initiatives to establish plantations of fast-growing tree species (mainly eucalyptus) around Sake and Kiwandja, for example. A more ambitious strategy is to make more electricity available to Goma. The super-rich American Howard Buffett Foundation is financing a major hydro-electric project to this end in Matebe, which was inaugurated by Joseph Kabila in December 2015. At the family level, the people of Goma have embraced solar power: there are more and more rooftop solar panels visible on both rich and middle-class homes but they are mainly used for lighting and charging mobile phones – not cooking.

Liboko is sceptical of the efficacy of the plantation initiatives that provide multiple-use wood to community groups. The trees are processed for construction and carpentry in addition to being used for *makala*. 'I don't see the point in all that. Demand for *makala* far exceeds supply so of course people will risk going into the park. Some traders import *makala* from Rwanda but that is a drop in the bucket. *Gomatraciens* don't even like Rwandan *makala* because it isn't as good as ours and we don't like their small bags which contain less than 50 kilos.'

Like many other rare and expensive resources, *makala* is consumed with parsimony – even in well-to-do families. Mothers, grandmothers, aunts, sisters and servants have come up with lots of different practices to get the most out of a bag of charcoal. The most obvious one is use of the improved cooking stove. Often associated with energy for development in the African Sahel, Latin America and Asia, development planners and environmental NGOs promoted the idea in Goma and it was accepted with little resistance. Awareness campaigns were widespread and the pragmatic people of Goma came to realise that a bag of *makala* lasts longer when using an improved stove compared with the traditional *brasero*. The message was simple: minimise heat loss from the burning charcoal. Local artisans were trained to make the simple device with recycled metal and clay and adapted the production format to the user's needs: for example, large versions exist for restaurants to cook large quantities of food at a time. Charcoal costs more in Goma today than in any other Congolese city, which helps explains Liboko's declaration that 'every household in Goma – even the poor ones – has at least one improved stove'.

A few residential areas in Goma do have a fairly reliable source of electricity, and here some families have freezers. They can prepare large quantities of food at one time and freeze it in individual portion sizes. They have developed a cooking technique conducive to cooking with very large pots. A mound of lava stones is built with a concave top on which the charcoal is placed. 'It's only in Goma that you see this,' says Liboko, 'because it is a miniature reproduction of the Nyiragongo volcano – with cone and crater – that looms over our city.' This is a widespread cooking technique that people have adapted according to their specific needs. 'In addition to being able to safely support large pots, women like this idea because the lava stones retain their heat for at least a few minutes even after the *makala* has burned to ashes.' Along the same lines, women also mix stones and charcoal in their *mbabula*. Women who simply do not have money to buy even a micro portion of *makala* resort to another solution: 'The really poor mothers sweep up *makala* dust and bits in markets and around depots and mix them with stones in their *mbabula*. It isn't easy to cook a meal that way but it is better than nothing.'

These different practices testify to the importance charcoal has for the average family in Goma. 'There isn't a woman here who isn't preoccupied with the cost of *makala*, even though it is the poorer ones who devote a bigger share of their budget to it.' Even Liboko himself, who handles bags of charcoal every day, says he is not immune to having to use it sparingly.

People see me covered in *makala* dust from head to toe and think that I have all I need. But they don't know what it is like for me. There are plenty of times when my depot is full but my supply at home has run out. I must make sure my paying customers have priority. You also need to remember that the *makala* in my depot doesn't belong to me. I'm just an intermediary between the owners and the buyers. When I depended on a depot owner in the past, I kept a keen eye on how he managed my *makala*. My suppliers do the same.

A NECESSARY EVIL

Liboko is thick-skinned about the way the people of Goma perceive *makala* traders. He knows that they recognise their work as crucial – '*makala* is life' – but at the same time they feel disdain for these men covered in black dust.

I don't care what people think. I'm happy to be earning my living by participating in an important part of daily life. There is neither shame nor pride in what I do because *makala* is a necessary evil. Rich folk look down on us but concede that they need us – even though at the same time they put us in the category of hustlers who do whatever they can to survive. Luckily, lots of poor souls like myself – and some middle-class people who haven't forgotten their humble origins – show us respect. They know that they can't live without us and sometimes even consider us as their friends.

Liboko is in a phase of self-doubt about his future in the *makala* business for both personal and regulatory reasons. 'I'm getting old and don't have the energy I used to. It's getting to be time to make way for the younger generation.' His vague plan is to get involved in the buying and selling of cheap consumer items. 'Profits will be lower but it won't be back-breaking and there will be no foreseeable risks to my physical safety.'

His exit strategy is also motivated by what he sees as emerging constraints on access to trees. 'Our activities are increasingly controlled, which is liable to making them more and more complicated. This results from greater efforts at clamping down on illegal charcoal production in the Virunga Park by international conservation NGOs, donors and the Congolese government agencies.' Liboko is well-aware of plans to improve the electricity supply to Goma but is sceptical of them materialising. 'There has been talk of Lake Kivu gas development – like in Rwanda – and hydroelectric projects, but who knows what it means. I don't know where people would get the money to buy electric stoves even if they wanted to. If that does happen, it would be another problem for us *makala* traders.' If locally appropriate alternative strategies for cooking energy do become available, it would be a good thing for the environment, concedes Liboko. 'But what will become of us *makala* professionals?' He is not worried about that yet, however, because Goma is still an over-whelmingly *makala*-dependent city.

CHAPTER 4

A STONECUTTER'S PARADISE

MBULA MATARI IN THE LAND OF THE VOLCANO

Nature's endowment to the region upon which Goma was built is a hard, black, rocky ground. It is nearly impossible to find a naturally level spot, which makes roadbuilding and house construction challenging. These topographical constraints, doubled with the problem of state neglect, have hardened the people who expect little from anyone but themselves. A long phase of insecurity in the region, sparked by the Rwandan genocide in 1994, pushed people from throughout the area into the perceived safer refuge of the city. Goma boomed in terms of demographic growth and spatial expansion. Forced to fend for themselves, people accepted whatever work opportunities the informal sector offered. These unskilled workers, empowered by their brawn and determination, are significant players in Goma's dynamism.

The eruption of the Nyiragongo volcano on 17 January 2002 dramatically transformed Goma's complexion. It was a natural catastrophe causing loss of life and massive destruction of property, but at the same time it sparked new opportunities. Pockets of relative prosperity now cover the traces of destruction as houses are rebuilt and streets are rehabilitated – in most cases in the very places that were blanketed with molten lava only a few years ago. Sandwiched between Lake Kivu, the Virunga National Park and Rwanda, the city hurriedly continues to fill the interstices of available building space: the people of Goma call their city *une ville en chantier* – a massive worksite.

Petrified lava is a handicap for some but a blessing for others. The people of Goma are expert in finding pragmatic uses for it. Most importantly, it is the building material used for house foundations and the walls that divide lots. Women use it to economise on *makala* by mixing it in their *braseros* and pumice is effective in cleaning one's calloused feet. Artists have adopted it too; it is impossible to stroll through the commercial areas of the city without seeing stone replicas of the region's endemic mountain gorilla. Blocks of lava, sometimes artistically carved or assembled, also serve as stands upon which street vendors present their wares.

Bula matadi translates as 'breaking stone' in the Kikongo language and has a deep historical connotation in the Congo. It was first associated with the forced labour inflicted upon the Congolese to construct the Leopoldville–Matadi railroad in the late nineteenth century. The locution gradually mutated into *mbula matari* as it became associated with the Belgian colonial administration. In other Congolese cities today, men with hammers and chisels produce building stones and gravel, often in stone quarries. But Goma has no specific stone quarry – the city itself is just a giant bed of lava that offers livelihood opportunities for a large number of men. Even though anyone can improvise as a lava carver, it is in fact a job that requires a certain amount of *savoir faire*. Using the strength of his biceps, where in other settings the work would be done with machines, the Goma stonecutter actively participates in the metamorphosis of the landscape.

TWO AMONG MANY

Mituga Bahizire was born of Bashi parents in 1982 in the Maniema town of Kalima, where the Kivu Mining Company (SOMINKI) owned a concession for the extraction of gold and cassiterite (the main ore of tin). 'When I was a kid, my mother let me do what I wanted to do and didn't care if I studied or not – so I dropped out of high school after just two years. I preferred playing football anyway and was a pretty talented left-winger despite being small.' Having broken his tibia in a stadium match in 2004, he gave up football, left Kalima the next year and went to Biseya to dig cassiterite on an artisanal basis with some friends. 'That's where I first learned to wield the pick and crowbar.' After two years, he became discouraged and gave that up because of the armed self-defence militia *Raia Mutomboki*. 'They were constantly taking advantage of us, pillaging our stuff and killing those who resisted. My life was worth more than cassiterite so I decided to leave – and decided to try my luck in Goma.'

Mituga knew how to cut lava because the work was not dissimilar to his previous artisanal mining experience. The transition was facilitated by other stonecutters from his ethnic group. 'Getting started wasn't difficult but the work itself is absolutely exhausting. Swinging a sledge-hammer and pickaxe is hard on your hands and arms; yanking at a crowbar is backbreaking. By the end of the day, I didn't have the energy to do anything and couldn't even feel my dust-covered body.' After one year of an exhausting rhythm, Mituga thought it was time to take a wife to help comfort him. His girlfriend Mamie – who knew what to expect because her father and brothers were also stonecutters – accepted his proposal.

Mituga ran into some difficulties in the beginning. 'I'd slave away cutting and making stacks of stone for sale only to get back the next morning to see them gone. I got into many fights with the local wise guys. With my steel-like muscles, I'd give them a good beating too – which got me into trouble with the police.' As fighting did not solve the problem, Mituga decided to stop cutting construction blocks for sale and work only when he received a specific commission. Most jobs were digging septic wells and trenches for water and electricity conduits. He earned enough money to build his own modest home and take care of his wife and four children, who all go to school – a priority for Mituga. 'I missed out on life by not knowing how to read and write; I want better for my kids.'

Kambale Celestin, a Nande and Mituga's partner and his junior by four years, grew up at the foot of Mount

Ruwenzori in the town of Mutwanga. He never knew his father, a driver who was killed when his lorry overturned on the road between Beni and Kisangani at Mufutabangi. His mother had a difficult time raising him with his sister but was able to get him through school. After two unsuccessful attempts, he got his high school diploma in mechanical engineering on the third try when he was twenty. 'I wasn't spoiled as a kid and thought at the time that a degree would help.' Despite his father's accident, he wanted to become a lorry driver too. His mother, however, vetoed that idea, which led him to try his hand at gold mining in Ituri's Mambasa forest.

> I thought that I'd be able to get rich quick but it didn't take me long to wake up. I worked hard but ended up with little to show for it. Artisanal gold mining is a racket and I was taken advantage of, first by the bosses who financed my entrance into a team, then by the buyers, and again by the authorities who are supposed to regulate the activity. I was disgusted by the environment. And if by chance you do find a rich vein, you're liable to be eliminated by your rivals. I stuck it out for ten months and then threw in the towel. With a few hundred dollars in my pocket, I went back to live with my mother, helping her out with her farm work.

That chapter of his life did not last long: the region was going through major episodes of conflict and at twenty-four he was press-ganged into a rebel group loyal to the Congolese Rally for Democracy. After ten months of soldiering, he escaped when his unit was heading for the Rumangabo military camp. He then sought refuge in Goma, where one of his late father's sisters, happy to see him alive, took him in. He stayed with her for two months but he did not want to abuse the woman's hospitality. 'She was struggling herself and I didn't want to be a burden. At my age I should have been supporting her, not the opposite.' Finding odd jobs as a fee collector on a taxi-bus, monitor of a water distribution installation and barman, he was eventually able to rent his own studio and save some money. With a small amount of capital to invest, he opened a public telephone boutique, where he also bought and sold foreign currency.

An inveterate bachelor, Celestin is not averse to spending his money on clothes, good food and an occasional night out. The rest of his earnings go to rent and helping both his mother, who still lives in Mutwanga, and his aunt in Goma, who he visits as often as he can. 'I'm not ready to have a family because it seems to be an additional worry for someone like me who has to live by his wits. But I have to admit that there are moments when I'm envious of Mituga, who was able to overcome his fear of family obligations.'

Celestin and Mituga met in 2008. Mituga was one of Celestin's regular customers, changing currency and sometimes borrowing money. These two young men with very different backgrounds became friends and Mituga perceived that Celestin had the potential to be a useful partner. Celestin had recently been robbed and was ready to change jobs once again. The conversation between them went like this: 'Hey, Celestin, what's the matter? You look worried today.'

'Ah, Mituga, my friend. You may think that I earn plenty of money when you see the stacks of banknotes on my makeshift stand, but you don't know the half of it. Drunken soldiers took everything I had last night – over $500 that wasn't even mine. I have no idea how I'll ever pay that amount back. You always repay your loans to me on time so I guess your job isn't so bad.'

'Are you kidding me? I'm jealous of your fancy clothes and smart talk. With the dust caked on my calloused hands, I would never have thought of asking you to work with me – but maybe the time is right. Take a stab at it. The work is exhausting but it is low profile and you are your own boss. You'd pick it up in no time with your experience digging for gold up in Ituri. We would be a good team because, don't forget, you need two fingers to crush a flea.'

'Why not? When a lion can't catch an antelope, it nibbles on grass.'

READY FOR HARD LABOUR

Without any other reasonable option, Celestin accepted Mituga's offer. Dynamic and determined to take charge of their destinies, they are proud to have been able to transcend the ethnic cleavages 'that complicate this city where tribalism reigns'. They accept that their skills are modest

but see that, with every day's work, they are participating in changing the face of the city, along with others
like them. 'Our office is a scrap of land in the open air
that needs to be levelled. The job – which requires super-
human strength – is to mould that land. Elsewhere, this
transformation would be done with dynamite, mechanical graders, bulldozers, backhoes and dump trucks. Here
we do it with sledgehammers, pickaxes and crowbars.'

Celestin admits that he had to prepare himself psychologically before embracing his new vocation, given that
he had heard it was going to be torture for his body. 'The
money and flexibility were like carrots in front of the
stick.' Mituga was able to come up with other arguments.
'You are not going to be like a sitting duck on the street
with your stacks of francs; no one is going to look at you
with envy when they see you covered in dust, so who is
going to rob you now? You can use my tools and even
the authorities don't see any reason to hassle us stonecutters.' Celestin's contribution to the partnership was
a major boost to Mituga. 'His intellectual French and
smooth talking during negotiations opened doors that
were previously closed to me.'

Friends before starting to break stones together, their
relationship solidified over time. Mituga has a little rental
house in his compound that he offered to his friend for
free. Celestin, however, insisted on paying for it. Mituga's
wife cooks for Celestin too. 'To not upset Mamie, I agreed
to eat her delicious stews, meats, vegetables and beans
– but I pay Mituga for them without her knowing. She

would be insulted were she to learn this.' Those expenses are deducted from their shared earnings. 'It took me a while before I was comfortable accepting kindness and generosity because I consider myself to be ferociously independent.'

Steady work and frugally managed spending allowed them to save enough money to buy a Chinese-made motorbike. It was a breakthrough for them because, with the motorbike combined with mobile phones (which not many of their rivals have), they were able to get to prospective worksites fast. Their modus operandi is simple but efficient. Mituga heads out to new worksites early in the morning while Celestin uses the motorbike as a taxi, also keeping his eyes open for opportunities. When one of them sees something, they meet, study the assignment and size up the potential client. 'I do the talking,' says Celestin, 'because Mituga is clumsy, nervous and intransigent.' When an agreement is reached – which is rarely written down – they get moving. 'Both our rivals and clients tend to be unscrupulous so I rush off home on the motorbike to get the tools while Mituga waits at the worksite to make sure no one comes along with a lower price.'

Payment conditions vary with the job. An advance of between a tenth and a quarter of the total is generally requested before commencing the work – depending on the volume and complexity. The arrangements are made between Mituga and Celestin and the client without any involvement from municipal agents. As elsewhere in

DRC, urban development is taking place without urban planning. 'Here in Goma we build first and worry about permits after,' says Celestin with a wink.

IT'S THE HEAD
THAT BREAKS STONE

Mituga and Celestin are both short in stature and rather thin, without the bulging biceps that one would expect from men exerting the hard physical labour needed to dig septic wells and break stone for other infrastructure and construction initiatives. Mituga emphasises an unexpected attribute: 'It's the head that breaks stone, not muscle. Lava needs to be treated with respect. You need to cajole it before it accepts being broken into bits.'

Mituga initiated his friend in the art of breaking lava on a house construction project in 2010. The first client of their association, the friend of a relative of Celestin, had just acquired a plot measuring 30 metres by 40 in the Ndosho district. There were few houses there then, a pivotal moment when open land rapidly transformed into a densely populated residential settlement. When the owner first invited them to his plot, they discovered a rough, rocky, black, uneven no man's land that had never been cultivated or built on. 'Plenty of work and pockets full of money,' whispered one to the other.

The owner had a clear idea of how much he was willing to pay, what needed to be done and when the work was to be finished. The primary task was to completely level a patch of 20 metres by 15 upon which the house was to be built – by other workers. Thanks to his experience and cunning, Mituga was able to influence the owner on where exactly the house should go, employing false arguments that the work was more difficult than it appeared. 'Mituga is an honest man,' according to Celestin, 'but in this line of work a little bit of trickery can make the difference between good money and better money.' While the client knew that there were plenty of strong arms looking for work, Mituga and Celestin reminded him that there are lots of houses under construction. It is indeed neither a seller's nor a buyer's market. Both parties know the approximate cost for a job such as this one, based on the number of square metres and the nature of the topography. Mituga and Celestin agreed to do the work in such a way as to recycle the broken chunks of lava so that they could serve as the house's foundations. They settled upon a total of $450 to be paid in three instalments: a third up front, a third when the job was half done and the remainder upon completion – three weeks start to finish. The negotiation process was facilitated by the fact that both Celestin and the client are from the same ethnic group.

On the first day at the site, Mituga taught Celestin how to understand the hardened lava bed by tapping all over the designated work area with a light hammer. This was an important initial step because it determined what tools to use and how. Mituga is self-taught in the study of lava and, according to Celestin, 'has some kind of quasi-mystical relationship with it. When it resists, he talks to it and then the problem solves itself.' The next day, they were ready to get the real work under way and were equipped with the tools of the trade: pickaxes, 8 and 10 kilo sledgehammers, chisels, crowbars and recycled lorry leaf springs to use as wedges. 'Luckily we knew someone who lived nearby who agreed to look after our tools at night. Transporting them back and forth would have been difficult and leaving them at the site unattended was not an option because of thievery.'

After a few days of indefatigable enterprise, a portion of the land was level, and in a far corner stood the neatly stacked chunks that would be used for the foundations. Their exchanges are laconic while at work but the jibber-jabber picks up on the way home. 'Starving and exhausted, we can still muster up the energy to crack a few jokes,' they say in unison. After the scheduled three weeks, the foundation area was completely transformed into a level plane, contrasting sharply with the rest of the lot. The owner could therefore start construction. Satisfied with the result, he paid the third and final instalment.

Both Celestin and Mituga expend a lot of effort generating new work, but sometimes they just sit idle. Conversely, there are times when they are on more than one job at a time, which can lead them to recruit day labourers – 'muscle', they call them. 'Even in our sector,' says Mituga, 'the rules of hierarchy have to be respected. And I don't mind being called boss when the opportunity arises. Last year we had twenty jobs, each one lasting around ten days.' Some of their assignments are a result of good reports given by satisfied clients. There have been only a few occasions when there were disagreements about the quality of the work or the payment. 'The problems we did encounter were either with soldiers or political authorities, so we don't bother working with them anymore,' adds Celestin. At one point Mituga had the fleeting idea of establishing a lava workers' association but was quickly disillusioned by the lack of interest. 'Most stonecutters just want to work alone and live from one day to the next. They'll continue to live like dogs because of their ignorant attitudes.'

Respecting the rules of basic hygiene is difficult in Goma because of water management deficiencies. The first problem is access to water (official distribution is woefully insufficient) followed by used water treatment. State neglect, rapid unplanned urbanisation and the nature of the topography overlap, resulting in the absence of underground water conduits and sewers. These concerns translate into a prosaic household priority – the toilet. As Goma toilets are very rarely connected to a supply or evacuation system, the Goma solution is that men like Mituga and Celestin are hired to dig what is locally referred to as a sceptic well – basically a hole in the ground somewhere on the lot encased in a hut-like structure. Private operators with tank lorries are available to pump out the waste; other families pour large quantities of diesel fuel into the well to dissolve the waste. 'The depth of the well is proportional to the depth of the client's pocket,' add Mituga and Celestin, who consider themselves experts in digging these wells …

The plot was small and the house took up most of it. The corner designated for the well and the hut measured three metres by five; the hole was supposed to be two metres by four and two and a half metres deep. We started with a pickaxe and continued with our crowbars and hammers. The lava was so hard before getting very far down that we had to resort to other techniques – even the lorry leaf springs that we use as chisels to get into the smallest interstices weren't enough. We made a concoction of laundry detergent, kitchen salt and used motor oil, poured it into the lava and set it ablaze. The heat weakened the lava which facilitated further digging. The operation took us a whole month.

WE'VE STOPPED DREAMING

Goma's ongoing spatial expansion is a seemingly unstoppable process – but one challenged by multiple factors. Neither the inhospitable physical topography nor insecure land rights nor administrative hassles are strong enough to dampen the population's frenetic building spree, because – in addition to the robust urban pull of Goma – the desire to live in one's own home is a powerful driver. All sorts of people and trades contribute to the building of the city but the stonecutter plays a special role. Covered in black dust – like the city itself – and wielding their rudimentary tools, they reflect the local logic of resiliency and surprise. 'What other twenty-first-century city is being built with hand tools?' The question does not bother Mituga and Celestin, who have accepted their simple lifestyles and the physical drudgery of their destinies. They claim to be satisfied and serene about the future. 'Our work is irreplaceable in Goma – at least for the time being – and we have a solid friendship in this environment where inter-ethnic rivalries poison human relationships. Goma is a dangerous place but we don't worry about that.' Without hopes of upward social mobility, they focus on day-to-day survival, realising that cultivating unrealistic ambitions would likely lead to disappointment. 'We've stopped dreaming, but as long as we have our health, friendship and tools, we'll get by one way or another.'

CHAPTER 5

GOMA'S PUBLIC HEALTH CHALLENGES

FROM TRAUMA TO WHITE JACKET

Health and well-being in Goma suffer from conditions imposed by nature and by man. Natural risks such as earthquakes, volcanic eruptions and toxic gas pockets (*mazukus*) overlap with ongoing security and political problems, which exacerbate the already low level of human development. Goma's health needs are therefore somewhat different than those in other Congolese cities. Helping the population from a medical perspective is a challenge that the government is unable to cope with – even with the significant support it receives from international partners.

A host of factors have had a negative impact on the entire range of medical services. In Goma's rural hinterland, conflict has scattered families. Fear of militias and armed rebel groups forced people to abandon their agricultural activities – their sole source of income – augmenting their vulnerability and hunger. As these people flocked to Goma, food supplies dwindled; the pre-existing urban population had to share a smaller amount of food with the newcomers. The few peasants who refused to leave their villages hid in the forest but were unable to avoid attacks, sexually transmitted diseases after rape, and diseases caused by problems such as malnutrition and unsafe drinking water. Malaria ravaged these physically exhausted displaced men, women and children. Reports of rape and young boys press-ganged into fighting forces were widespread: it was generally acknowledged that both rebels and government soldiers had a hand in committing atrocities.

Insecurity, powerlessness and uncertainty lead people to distinguish between imminent danger and abstract risks. 'Risk is less of a fear than danger. The first you run, the second makes you run,' say the youth of the region. The physically unthinkable and the morally reprehensible have become commonplace in the fight to stay alive in this environment, where no one knows what new trauma tomorrow may bring. Why worry about a hypothetical sickness that could be caused by drinking unsafe water or eating spoiled food? Recourse to prostitution and therefore potential exposure to HIV/AIDS in order to buy food for dinner follows the same logic.

These attitudes and behaviours testify to the precariousness of health and sanitation. The decline of public education and inadequate state service provision reinforce this vulnerability. Schools, administration, churches and health services – all under pressure – are no longer in a position to support health education: basic rules are no longer taught, and they are respected even less. The demographic pyramid is another challenge: the city's population is young, fertile and not particularly amenable to family planning options – which, in any event, are poorly organised, inadequately available and cost-prohibitive for many women. These converging dynamics have turned Goma into a medical, social and sanitation conundrum. What do people do when they fall ill or have an accident? The gap between growing healthcare needs and the capacity of an already strained system to respond is a dilemma for doctors such as Chantal Sasolele.

'We have the skills and the good will to help our patients but we don't have the means to save all of them.' Sporting a white jacket and a smile, Doctor Chantal Sasolele sits neatly behind her little uncluttered work table in the paediatric clinic Tumaini Letu ('Our Hope' in Swahili), in the Notre Dame d'Afrique parish. 'My little visitors call me Mama Chantal,' she explains before telling the story of why she chose to become a doctor.

My vocation came to me in the aftermath of the 1994 drama of Rwandan refugees. They were flooding into the city. It was impossible to do anything. Sanitary conditions were worse than what you could imagine – and then came the cholera epidemic. People were dying left and right. For the first time in my life I saw a corpse – but not just one, hundreds of dead bodies all over the place. I was just a kid, so badly shaken up – I still remember the nightmares they gave me.

To avoid the risk of contamination from cholera, Chantal's father moved the family to his native village of Bunyuka, near Butembo. There, she was enrolled in a boarding school run by Catholic sisters that still trains primary school teachers today. But traumatised by what she had seen in Goma, she was unable to concentrate on her studies and ended the year with the poorest results of the whole class. 'That was unimaginable for my father but my mother figured out that it was a direct result of the human tragedy I had witnessed. She wasn't surprised because my teacher had already told her that I was suffering from some kind of fear of death.' In a school play, the teacher asked Chantal to play the role of a *munganga* (healer or doctor). Offering the part to her, the teacher explained that doctors help people not to die. 'They snatch them away from the clutches of death,' she said. 'When I heard that, and thinking about all those corpses, I knew what I would be when I grew up.'

During the summer holidays of that unsuccessful school year, Chantal's parents decided to head back to Goma. The family was fairly well-off and lived in a comfortable house that her father was able to build with the money he earned while working as a schoolteacher in the Central African Republic. Chantal returned to her previous school and was reunited with her classmates – all of them, that is, except her best friend, who had succumbed to cholera. 'Driven by my dream of becoming a doctor, I studied hard, getting through primary school, secondary school and getting my high school diploma in 2004. I realised that I was luckier than other children and appreciated the fact that both my parents were educated and concerned about my future.'

Diploma in hand, and thanks to the presence of a local university with a medical curriculum, Chantal's dream was taking form. Her friends suggested that she would get a better education in Kinshasa or abroad but she had set her mind on the University of Goma (UNIGOM). 'I didn't care that UNIGOM wasn't prestigious. First and foremost I just wanted to become a doctor and have a blouse with my name embroidered on the breast pocket. I'd find ways to be a good doctor afterwards.' Having graduated from medical school in 2010, she volunteered in various capacities to reinforce her skills until she found a position. These voluntary roles included internships at the Protestant hospital Communauté Baptiste au Congo de Virunga, Goma's General Hospital and the Salvation Army – internships that were necessary before she was eligible to take the Hippocratic Oath and receive her registration number from the National Counsel for the Order of Doctors. But with all this to her credit, she was still without paid work. An uncle, also a doctor and working at the Nyakunde hospital in Ituri, got her another unpaid internship which lasted eighteen months. 'Finally, I was offered my first salary as a doctor by a World Bank-funded project in Masisi.'

Dr Sasolele started her assignment in Masisi as a general practitioner but after a few months was asked to take charge of epidemiological surveillance in rural communities. 'I worked together with a nurse gathering statistical data and carrying out some basic exams (thick blood smears, scratch tests, stool examinations ...). I wasn't supplied with any pharmaceutical products and there were no clinics in the area so my work was frustrating. Why issue prescriptions that would remain unfilled?' Upon entering a village, Chantal would seek out the chief and explain her mission. It would be the chief who would then ask the heads of households to explain to the *maman munganga* whatever problems they may be suffering from. With her stethoscope around her neck, Chantal would start her examinations, which usually took place outdoors as there were no health clinics in these villages. For reasons of discretion, the adults would keep away from public consultations but arranged to see the doctor privately if they needed treatment. Reluctant at first, the children eventually came willingly – especially because they could see that she wasn't giving shots. 'I really got to enjoy working with these children who warmed my heart with their trust. In these poor rural areas their well-being tends to be neglected by adults. The desire to specialise in paediatrics came to me in these villages.'

On one of her rounds, Chantal met Gustave, a young economist who was distributing veterinary vaccinations on behalf of a local NGO. Chantal, who was testing people while Gustave tested cattle, had frequent random encounters with him. Gustave was struck by this energetic young doctor who had embraced her vocation with so much enthusiasm. The two university graduates, working in and discovering a difficult environment – and both Nande too – had lots to talk about, including their plans for the future. They quickly decided to marry and returned to Goma to organise their union according to the traditions of their families, who both 'willingly blessed the idea'. Chantal does not hesitate when it comes to taking decisions. Their engagement period was short; they were married less than a year after their first meeting and rented a house in Katindo. Shortly afterwards, they built their own home and then came the children: Gaëlle (born in 2011) and Josépha (2013). 'Work and family go together for me. Above all else I'm a doctor, then I'm a wife and mother. And I still consider myself my parents' little girl and the sister of my siblings.'

A DOCTOR'S DAILY GRIND

The medical system in DRC is theoretically regulated by the state – specifically the Ministry of Health. The national territory is subdivided into health zones; there is a legal framework and a range of health institutions – such as the more important general referral hospitals and the smaller rural dispensaries. Healthcare professionals, however, are highly critical of the gap between theory and reality. 'These bureaucracies are no more than parasites. Doctors like me are in constant conflict with the health administrations because they do not fulfil their role of policy orientation or finance. Their neglect has facilitated the privatisation of the health sector on the one hand, and the exaggerated involvement of health NGOs on the other. The state is clearly not doing its job.'

Like many other Congolese doctors, Chantal works in three different types of medical establishment – public, international and private. She juggles her time between the public Tumaini Letu clinic, the Kyeshero women's hospital, which was set up and funded by the Clinton Foundation to treat traumatised rape victims from the eastern Congo conflicts, and the private Afia medical association. 'They all have their specificities about how they organise our services, the nature of the equipment and supplies, and the way they treat patients.'

Tumaini Letu is Chantal's main base and she receives a monthly state salary for her practice there. Arriving at 8 am, she puts on her white smock and starts her rounds, checking on her young patients. She can spend anywhere between thirty minutes and an hour and a half with them depending on their needs. When that is done, she returns to her sparsely equipped and furnished office to examine new patients – up to thirty a day. 'The sick little kids I see represent the tip of the iceberg. There are plenty that I never get to help because their parents don't have the two dollars we require to register here. There are so many relatively innocuous pathologies that kill children in Goma even though they could easily be diagnosed and treated.' Water-borne intestinal diseases, malaria and respiratory problems are notable examples. 'Filling prescriptions is another drama for us. I can issue a prescription but not the medicine. Nor can I control if a medicine is being taken properly. Lots of parents don't have money to buy pharmaceutical products, and, if they do, often, out of ignorance, they don't respect the recommended dosage.'

The consultation–examination–prescription routine can be interrupted when there are emergencies. More often than not, patients arrive when it is already too late. 'These situations are painful for me because we are so underequipped we can't do much to help. The only thing to be done is sign the death certificate. Telling a parent that their child has passed away is a difficult responsibility. I do it myself but many of my colleagues delegate that heart-breaking moment to their assistants.' On a day like that, Chantal goes straight home after work and nothing can separate her from her own daughters, who she pampers to console herself. 'Gustave has learned to detect my moods and does what he can to calm me down. By bedtime, we hope for a decent night's sleep and a better next day. I'm grateful for the good husband I found. He doesn't interfere with my career even though he has demanding responsibilities himself. All in all we have nothing to complain about.'

'I find tremendous satisfaction in dilly-dallying with the children in my ward. These kids, most under ten, can be so good-humoured when they start to recover from an illness or accident; and talkative too – often expressing themselves more freely to me than to their own mothers.' Her satisfaction, nevertheless, is embittered by her powerlessness – the population's needs are overwhelming and the system dysfunctional.

Tumaini Letu suffers from the same kind of obstacles as other public services in the DRC: absence or misappropriation of subsidies and operating budgets, insufficient and outdated equipment, and low salaries. In this already inauspicious work environment, Chantal shares a work space with a large group of paediatricians, which means she cannot leave anything in it. She therefore has to carry her own material (such as a thermometer and stethoscope) in her doctor's bag. Rubber gloves, syringes, bandages, disinfectants and other such items are included in the prescription to be purchased by the patient – a widespread practice in the DRC. For poor parents of sick children, these costs might well dissuade them from going through with the treatment.

When an ill-equipped or underfunded clinic is unable to carry out certain examinations or treatments, the patient is referred to another institution. This leads to what Chantal flags as an ethical problem. 'My colleagues tend to refer a patient to an institution from which they can expect a commission. This isn't right. The choice of another medical institution should be based on the patient's needs and capacity to pay – not on the amount of the doctor's kickback.'

The privatisation of the public health sector is a paradoxical trend that results from the desire of doctors to help poor patients while generating revenues for underfunded public institutions. It is an intermediary option between an inefficient public sector and private institutions that are beyond the reach of ordinary people. In concrete terms, fees earned in the private wing of a public institution are reinjected into the overall operating budget. Managers of public sector institutions saw the emergence of a category of people suited to this kind of hybrid arrangement as an opportunity. The trend, however, is perceived as being controversial within the medical profession. Some doctors disapprove because they argue that it exonerates the government from assuming its responsibilities. Others, like Chantal, consider it to be socially pertinent. 'Under this arrangement, anyone can receive basic treatment in Goma. It isn't like that in Kinshasa, where hospital staff pay scant attention to poor patients. That's also one of the great things about Goma – at the neighbourhood level, at school or at church, people who have the means to do so try to help those who are less fortunate.'

Chantal has had many gratifying experiences during her professional involvement in Tumaini Letu (where the following episode took place) and elsewhere.

A little girl of around five years old came to the centre with her mother to visit one of our patients. As I was coming out of the visiting ward, all of a sudden the girl grabbed my legs shouting: 'Mama *munganga*! Mama Chantal.' I was taken aback until her mother emerged and then I recognised both of them. When I was working in Masisi, I treated the little girl for measles, without having any idea what became of her. Measles kills young children in our environment. The fact that she survived – and recognised me – filled me with joy.

Notwithstanding the obvious shortcomings in the small public centre where she works, Chantal feels comfortable there, particularly from an ethical perspective. 'It's an environment in which the Hippocratic Oath has meaning, where I can really help vulnerable people.' She has the insight to make a comparison because internationally funded institutions sometimes solicit her services. 'Kyeshero and Heal Africa [the clinic for expatriates and well-to-do Congolese] are mirages in the desert,' according to Dr Mbusa, one of Chantal's colleagues. They see them as an imported health model motivated by the humanitarian logic of acting at any price in situations of distress. 'They are clean and well stocked with basic medical products and have state-of-the-art equipment; patients are cared for correctly and doctors decently paid. Their sponsors have the leveraging power to attract millions of dollars. The work environment is friendly and full of expatriate doctors anxious to share their expertise. I learned a lot from them about emergency care and new medical technology.' But what may be good for the doctors is not necessarily good for the patients. In Chantal's opinion, 'the model doesn't work' because 'it was designed in a faraway country without thinking that lots of people are excluded from these medical enclaves because they can't afford the fees or they do not fulfil the inflexible admissions criteria'. There have been hundreds of well-intentioned medical interventions in eastern DRC over the past twenty years, some more successful than others. Chantal echoes a view shared my many of her

Congolese and international colleagues: 'We know that the current arrangement is far from perfect – definitely makeshift – but if we can save even a single life, then the investment is morally justified.'

The Kyeshero hospital for traumatised rape victims is an unsettling place for Chantal and her co-workers. 'These women have lost their *joie de vivre*. We explain to them over and over that they are not responsible for what happened but it doesn't sink in. It is exceptional in Congo to see women who don't find pleasure in just being together, probably because they feel guilty.' It was in this setting that Chantal experienced the worst day in her career.

Natalie, a nineteen-year-old girl, just gave birth to a baby conceived in rape. The newborn was in good health and I had the impression that the mother would be able to start a new chapter focused on her child. But I got the shock of my life when entering her room for a routine check and discovered a horror story. Natalie had suffocated her baby with a pillow and then hung herself. She left a note expressing her anguish to the effect that the baby reminded her of the rapist father so she was incapable of accepting it. I was a total wreck for two weeks after the tragedy, realising that the encouragements that I had tried to give the girl had in fact rekindled the hatred she had for her attacker. By killing her baby, she was wiping him out too. Life had lost all meaning for her.

In addition to medical competence, bolstered by the empathy she has for her patients, Chantal also has the talent to navigate successfully in Goma's health provision marketplace. While her heart is in Tumaini Letu, she is not averse to selling her skills to private clinics such as Afia. Critical but ambiguous, she considers them as 'businesses like supermarkets where a doctor sells health services as if they were merchandise. At the same time, the managers of these establishments have to be professional because an inaccurate diagnosis, poor treatment or any other mistake can ruin their reputation, sending patients to the competition.' Chantal has her own agenda with these medical 'supermarkets'. It is a means for her to earn extra money, to be exposed to relatively modern resources, and – potentially – to establish her own clientele because she is planning to open her own clinic: 'one where the patient will be placed at the heart of therapeutic action'. On good terms with her male and female colleagues and respected for her expertise in paediatrics, her services are regularly sought after. 'Men and women doctors all get along well in my circle – there are no gender rivalries or complexes. Some people prefer female paediatricians; some are more comfortable with male gynaecologists – those are secondary considerations for me.'

WITCH DOCTOR OR MEDICAL DOCTOR?

Medical doctors are obviously key protagonists in health service provision in Goma but they are not the only ones.

Traditional healers (*nganga*) also play a role. Both are necessary for the population but for different reasons. 'The landscape is also overrun with charlatans who present themselves as doctors, which is a calamity when it comes to performing abortions, for example,' laments Chantal.

> The involvement of the patient is essential to healing but people shop around, weighing up different factors before making a decision. For someone who is sick and wants the suffering to end, the perceived subtleties between a real doctor and an imposter, a medical assistant or a nurse, are trivial questions. The key factor in a city like Goma – where people are poor and do not have subsidised health programmes – is getting better quickly by spending the least amount of money.

Chantal is open-minded about holistic therapeutic approaches because she functions in a complex socio-medical environment where belief systems influence choices. To be a good paediatrician, she needs to understand the psychological drivers of patients and their families. 'People do not believe that pain, sickness and suffering are normal states. They are perceived as being punishments resulting from a sin that was committed or a curse sent by a rival or anyone with a grudge.' The very first phase in a healing process is spiritual. For some Christian believers, this means turning to God, praying and organising deliverance ceremonies and night-time vigils. In this sense, priests, preachers and other religious intermediaries are healers. Others seek the council of ancestors, relying on the assistance of witchdoctors (*bandoki*) and mediums to pacify the evils spirits that are punishing them. In many cases, the decision to see a doctor follows a phase of doubt, hesitation and procrastination.

> A sick person just waits to see if the problem will go away by itself. Then he'll go to a pharmacist and try some random medicines. In DRC, pharmacists are unlicensed and uncontrolled so access to pharmaceutical products is easy. Goma's Virunga market has a large drugs section where products are sold under the blazing sun and without instructions. If none of this helps, asking friends and family who have had a similar problem follows, with perhaps recourse to the same treatment.

When conditions warrant recourse to the formal medical sector, people usually try to find a friend – or a friend of a friend – who can give some free professional advice. This depends on one's social network and the nature of the illness and its stigma. There is less hesitation about consulting a professional for a skin infection than for suspected symptoms of HIV/AIDS. 'People wind up coming to hospital when they are already pretty far gone. The potions and concoctions they may have ingested during the procrastination period aggravate the situation. It's no mystery that sick people brought to hospital

often don't get out alive. The image of the health professional is tarnished because we are then accused of being
incompetent.'

The association between certain socio-medical problems
and the fact that Goma has become a multi-ethnic and
multicultural city is a concern for the medical profession. 'Goma is a melting pot for people with significantly
different backgrounds but with violence and suffering
as common denominators. This pushes people to drastic
actions out of ignorance and jealousy.' Chantal is referring
here specifically to common attitudes about witchcraft.
'Modern medicine can't do much in the face of powerful
belief systems. I have heard all kinds of stories relating
to spells being cast on patients. When married couples
cannot have children, for example, they tend to believe that
the problem is a curse and not a medical issue.' Another
major socio-medical reality that puts doctors in a difficult
position is the widespread practice of poisoning. 'This is
a shameful and widespread practice. No one is immune.
It happens between disgruntled colleagues, sexual rivals
and unhappy business associates. It even happens within
families – if, for example, someone with a job isn't sharing
enough.' Victims tend not to consult a medical doctor
after being poisoned: 'The cure is dealt with by healing
specialists. Even doctors who have been poisoned go to
them, which proves that it is a problem subject to cultural
sensitivities on which doctors have little impact.'

Chantal is a woman who gives life by bringing children
into the world and a doctor who cures diseases and saves

lives. 'The medical profession offers me the possibility of developing my human and professional potential to the fullest.' Her white jacket is a symbol of community engagement and commands respect given the enormous health needs in Goma. 'Where human life is constantly under threat, those who help others in the cradle-to-tomb cycle are treated with dignity. I feel it every day when people – who do not even know me – give me a respectful nod when they perceive I'm a doctor.' In the space between birth and death, Chantal is convinced that she and her colleagues can help people survive, develop and take their lives in their own hands. Closely embedded in her environment, for Chantal, the idea of migrating to a potentially more propitious setting such as South Africa (where many Congolese doctors have prospered), Europe or America is not a consideration. 'I'm proud of my work, my community and my city and I'm grateful for having been born in the DRC. Thanks to God's help and our strength we will overcome our problems.'

CHAPTER 6

A PRAGMATIC HUMANITARIAN

BORN TO HELP

Eric Kyungu, born in the Ituri city of Beni in 1975, started doing volunteer work when he was a high-school student. His first assignment was cleaning Beni's central market after having joined the non-profit association Ecologists' Partnership for the Protection of Nature – SEPRONA. His day started at 4.30 am – every day except Sunday. 'I'd be out there sweeping and picking up market rubbish with a few friends from 5 to 8 am because we thought helping out the community was a good thing to do. Although we were officially volunteers, we did receive a few francs from the market association – in addition to getting good deals from the vendors who appreciated our help.' He admits, however, that the desire to help was part of a strategy to create his own social image. 'Promoting one's self as an ecologist and a volunteer was an excellent means to get in good with the host of NGOs active around Beni who at the time were looking for workers. It is a recommendation in itself and a way to get into the NGO circle.' This was a first example of Eric's long-term vision and his capacity to plan. 'I wasn't ashamed of cleaning the market stalls, even though some people looked down on me for doing so. Others were even jealous of the small advantages we derived but without admitting it. They were either lazy or vain, but I didn't give them that much thought.'

In 1996, Beni was taken by Laurent-Désiré Kabila's Alliance of Democratic Forces for the Liberation of Congo-Zaire (AFDL), just as Eric received his high school diploma. Lacking specific plans for the future, he gave serious thought to joining the famous *kadogo* fighting unit along with some friends. His family, however, adamantly opposed this idea and decided to get him out of Beni. Eric's older brother, Claude, lived in Goma, so his parents arranged for him to go and live under his roof. 'I didn't have any strong political views and acquiesced to my parents' wishes.' Claude helped him register at a business school (the Institut Supérieur de Commerce), where he received his degree in accounting and business administration. While studying, he continued to cultivate his interest in community work. In 1996, Eric took an emergency first aid course organised by the Red Cross and received a certificate that allowed him to serve as a volunteer – mainly for road accidents. When the certificate was issued, he also got a membership card and equipment: uniform, boots, beret, scarf, canteen and a first aid kit. Free medical care came along with the package of benefits. Higher-ranking members received more benefits than the simple volunteers, so he ran for the presidency of the Red Cross's university committee. 'Thanks to the votes of classmates from the Beni area, I won.'

As president, Eric was exposed to a different perspective on the Red Cross. 'I had the fantastic opportunity of associating with expatriates in coordination meetings, where the work of the different Red Cross brigades was planned and budgeted.' This came to an end when he graduated, because the position was reserved for students. 'The Red Cross resident representative – a Norwegian nicknamed Viking – and I got along really well and he didn't want to lose me. I think he liked my willingness to help and my low-key personality.' Viking urged Eric to join the municipal committee of the Red Cross, which he did. This was in addition to his full-time position as an accountant at the Hotel Mont Goma, where he was hired shortly after graduation.

Upon Viking's recommendation, I was designated deputy secretary in the urban committee, which allowed me to continue sitting in on the coordination meetings. It wasn't easy combining Red Cross activities with my full-time job but it was worth it. In 2003, I was elected vice president of the North Kivu provincial committee, but as the president was also the director of the regional road infrastructure programme, he didn't have any time to devote to the Red Cross. I consequently acted as the de facto president, taking on responsibilities for organising meetings, interfacing with other NGOs, the provincial government and the urban committee.

These responsibilities transformed Eric from volunteer to humanitarian professional. 'It was an important phase for me personally – and for Goma, as hundreds of humanitarian NGOs established their headquarters here to help victims of the regional conflicts.' In his new role, Eric participated in three sorts of meetings: internal Red Cross ones, multi-partner meetings and coordination sessions between humanitarian organisations and the provincial government to respond to urgent situations.

> The ten years I spent at the helm of the provincial committee (from 2003 to 2013) was a school of life for me. The most important thing I learned is the value of human relationships – and to never underestimate them. Humanitarian and government networks opened up in front of me. People knew my name, in part because I was responsible for the Red Cross budget for the entire North Kivu province. I also did well financially during that decade. My lucky day came during an operation in a displaced persons camp at Kibata: it was there that I met the woman who was to become my wife and mother of my children. Jacquie was working as a nurse for Caritas – an important organisation of the Catholic Church. Her unfaltering energy to help victims was amazing. We married shortly after – in 2005.

Eric quit his job at the hotel two years later to set up his own chartered accounting office. 'The hotel environment was becoming dangerous for me because, as an accountant, I witnessed some shady dealings. I was even poisoned twice.' His decision was also motivated by the extent of his network: his clients were the directors of the humanitarian organisations he had been dealing with who required his services for external audits. 'I earned some serious money that way, but when a humanitarian urgency arose, I'd readily put on the cap of emergency care professional.'

Eric's luck took a turn for the worse in September 2013: new provincial committee elections were held and his bid was unsuccessful. After heading the committee for a decade, his ego did not allow him to stay on as a volunteer. His assessment of his long experience with the Red Cross is bittersweet – bitter because the end came against his will but sweet in terms of its rewards. He was able to buy land and build his home in Himbi. Some of the money was earned by accounting but the lion's share came from his humanitarian work. The primary reward for him is his social position. 'My doors are always open to brothers, sisters and other family members. As long as God gives me life, I'll struggle to help others – even people who are not from my ethnic group. The Red Cross taught me to offer help and I'm grateful for that lesson.'

UNDER FIRE

Even though Eric is largely upbeat about his own personal involvement in the humanitarian sector, he makes no attempt to mask its weaknesses. The United Nations Office for the Coordination of Humanitarian Affairs (OCHA) is the main coordination body in North Kivu and dates back to 1994. 'The logic is simple. Following the Rwandan genocide, more than 200 local, national and international NGOs flooded to Goma for humanitarian operations. From practically one day to the next the streets of Goma became congested with SUVs whose doors displayed nice clean logos. But the situation was chaotic and coordination was haphazard.' Eric's goodwill should not be confused with his lack of indulgence about how operations in the field were implemented. He admits to being dismayed by the attitudes and behaviours of some of his humanitarian counterparts and by policy deficiencies.

> My Congolese colleagues – like myself – have been extremely critical of the way the United Nations agencies deal with complex humanitarian situations such as the eastern Congo trauma. Efficient coordination does indeed depend upon hierarchy and control, but that is not enough when it comes to dealing with emergencies that require multiple levels of action. The big problem is the absence of coherent policies. Actions were taken on an ad hoc basis – case by case. The North Kivu situation is so complex that the approaches taken haven't really helped.

During the years when Eric was active in the sector, humanitarian agencies and NGOs made efforts to redress these problems through creative coordination actions – but with limited success. There were four approaches: 'One, each organisation had its own planning strategies; two, OCHA brought the different actors together once a week to share information about actions taken the previous week; three, thematic clusters (health, security, education, logistics …) met to discuss priorities and work on funding proposals; and last, the provincial government worked with the entire set of partners to identify priorities and strategies to deal with them.' These efforts could not, however, diminish the competition for funding. 'There were too many NGOs seeking financial support from a limited pool of donors for similar activities, leading to unspoken agendas.'

Eric experienced first-hand a coordination snafu in November 2011 when M23 rebels were fighting with Mai-Mai militias near Sake. 'People were displaced, deprived of shelter, food and water. The Red Cross provided water purification kits. International Solidarity did the exact same. But no efforts were taken to resolve the food supply problem. No efforts were made to deal with shelter. This was a blatant example of poor coordination.'

'Stressful but productive' is the phrase used by Eric to describe his experience in the humanitarian sector. Field operations gave him 'the craving for challenges'; to be a good humanitarian worker, 'you need to like people, have a solid dose of goodwill and be tenacious – and sometimes a little bit reckless'.

There have been many confrontations in North Kivu and half the time we don't know who is fighting who. We've gone through combat zones caring for the wounded without distinguishing what side they were fighting for – a basic Red Cross tenet. It sounds crazy but we often didn't grasp the danger lurking around us. To keep our sanity while in the throes of gathering dead bodies and dealing with victims of war, accidents and natural catastrophes, we'd chant our favourite refrain: 'Bearing arms is inhumane; our motto is mitigating suffering.'

Four events stand out in Eric's career. The first is the bombing of Goma by the Kinshasa government in a failed attempt to dislodge the occupying forces of the Congolese Rally for Democracy (RCD).

The bomber arrived around 8 pm on 2 August 1998 to destroy the airport, but the pilots mistook the streetlights of the street *kibarabara kya Majengo* for the lights along the airport's landing strip. By accident, they dropped their bombs in the heart of a densely populated neighbourhood, killing dozens of civilians, destroying property and wiping out public lighting. It was a struggle for us to recover the wounded and the dead in the near total darkness. When we were able to get victims to hospitals, the medical teams there were overwhelmed by the number of people requiring emergency treatment. I was already used to seeing dead and mutilated bodies, but the horror and magnitude of this tragedy was hard to cope with. I was revolted by the very sight of meat for days after.

Another 'discovery of absolute pure horror' was made when he was involved in relief operations during the occupation of Sake by the National Congress for the Defence of the People. 'Innocent civilians were hacked to death with machetes, perhaps to save bullets but more probably out of sheer savagery. There was a massive rape campaign and many women died from the brutality.' Some were infected with HIV and others became pregnant. 'It was hard for me to process this because I couldn't stop thinking that my own wife and children could have been the targets of this barbarity.'

Eric was also on the ground in April 2008 when a Hewa Bora jet overshot the landing strip and crashed into Birere in the middle of the day – a time when the district was crowded with shoppers, traders and shop-keepers. People died and buildings caught fire. 'It was impossible to stop the fire in this city without a fire brigade and without access to water. My powerlessness to help these people – and the stench of their scorched flesh – still haunts me.'

The litany continues with a story of a somewhat different nature – the taking of the city by the M23 between 15 and 21 November 2012. Eric was a first-hand observer of the inability of the national army troops to keep the Rwandan-backed rebels at bay. 'As the army fled to Sake, the population of Goma carried out their normal daily activities relatively undisturbed. There was little need for humanitarian assistance. The horror of this invasion was not one of brutality but of humiliation.'

Humanitarian aid sometimes helps, according to Eric, but he remains critical of a host of organisational drawbacks. 'They are not fixing the right problems. For the time being, they are necessary but not enough.' Actions do not always take local reality into account, particularly with respect to consultation: targeted beneficiaries are under-consulted and poorly understood, which translates into a wide gap between expected and actual results. 'Obliged to follow ill-adapted rules and regulations imposed by donors, project managers have become cynical. Instead of really helping, they are more concerned with budget absorption and respecting procedures elaborated abroad. Worse, problems are sometimes deliberately maintained by those who are supposed to solve them, supporting the stupid paradox of "no war, no work, no money".'

Another weakness results from the way in which young expatriate humanitarians with good intentions but little experience perceive the people of eastern Congo. 'We have the impression that they want to act at any cost, preferring imperfect operations to no operations at all.' This is typical of aid delivery systems that seek to address immediate problems without thinking about how to solve the deep-rooted causes. 'The system defends itself by saying that saving a single life is a justification in itself – but this justification is articulated for international public consumption – not for us.' The fact that small, local associations active in humanitarian relief have been eclipsed by large international NGOs is another of Eric's preoccupations.

The big NGO machine has steamrollered into the relief business, crushing the others while claiming all the credit and absorbing all the funding. This is unfortunate because our small structures correspond better to local needs and world views and their actions are motivated by the resolution of problems with and for the communities in need. Some of Goma's major problems are unemployment, limited access to credit, ethnic tension and low levels of human development. These problems cannot be solved by foreigners. Our own structures are far better suited to deal with them, even though they, too, have limited success to boast about.

Probably the best example of this reality is the way that religious institutions have evolved. In eastern Congo, Catholic, Protestant, Islamic and Pentecostal associations are all involved. 'They constitute a visible force in Goma in dealing with social priorities such as water supply, health services to displaced families, assistance to prison inmates and relief in emergency situations.' Eric's idealised vision for improved development in the region is based on better partnerships and respect. 'The big NGOs have the means to help us achieve what we want to do but don't have the means to do. This includes promoting small-scale private business and cooperatives, training workshops, formal and informal professional associations and neighbourhood community initiatives.' He emphasises, however, that this model of partnership would require careful management to avoid opportunist or fake local associations from dipping into the NGO funding stream without having the slightest intention of working once the money is made available. A related risk is that these unscrupulous associations – which are referred to as 'briefcase NGOs' in Congo – can undermine the whole process and therefore penalise the honest ones.

KIVU'S HUMANITARIAN BUSINESS

Humanitarian assistance channelled into the Congo – like other forms of aid – contributes to a cycle of dependency that is difficult to avoid. 'Actions help but they stifle individual and community initiatives. And when a project comes to an end, people are lost.' Eric's comment here relates to priorities that should be addressed by the government and administrative agencies, such as: capacity building and training; the supply of equipment to public service providers in the form of computers, office material and internet technology; resources for improved food security (seeds, modified plant types, fertilisers and small tools); road construction and maintenance; and health and education services.

United Nations peacekeeping actions are the most extreme example of the perverse side effects of external intervention, according to Eric. 'What has MONUSCO done to stabilise the region, even with all the billions of dollars eaten over the years? Not much. The stakes are just too complex in eastern Congo.' He was able to observe incoherent actions during his own field activities.

'The MONUSCO Indian contingent was stationed in close proximity to the M23 headquarters where notorious M23 leaders like Bertrand Bisimwa were based. Racketeering, systematic road tolls, pillaging and even summary executions took place under their noses without the least interference.' In another incident, two UN jeeps were stopped at the *Grande Barrière* border crossing into Rwanda with 2 tonnes of cassiterite: 'proof that MONUSCO Blue Helmets are active in the illegal trade of Congolese conflict minerals. Moreover, cases of sexual abuse of children by the Blue Helmets are common knowledge.' Relations between MONUSCO and local people are tense, and those with the government range from cordial to quite conflictual. A low point was when Kinshasa declared Scott Campbell, the UN bureau chief for human rights, *persona non grata* in DRC in October 2014 in the wake of his vocal criticism of the government.

Work in the Kibati, Lac Vert and Mugunga refugee camps around Goma provided a further example for Eric's litany of humanitarian paradoxes: in this case, that of a narrow-minded mandate. Refugees and internally displaced people (IDPs) were settled next to local residents who were just as poor and deprived as the newcomers. 'Despite their generosity towards the refugees and IDPs, they could not accept that the others received help from the international community while poverty was at their very own doorstep.' Eric echoed a complaint by a disgruntled mother near a camp: 'NGOs are giving out clean drinking water for free to the refugees but we have to look on and drink from the lake.' Situations like this lead to some startling reactions. 'Opportunists among local residents left their homes to register in the camps, expecting care and benefits. But they also discovered the absurdity of aid. Some of the types of food they were given are not part of their dietary habits and they didn't want them. They wound up at the city's markets for sale or exchanged for products they were more familiar with.' The same markets were also known to be stocked with bags of food pilfered from international donations.

The plethora of aid, development and relief humanitarians in Goma has created some clearly identifiable advantages for the city – notably by providing work for the population. They need 'focal points', resource people, managers, logistics staff, accountants, secretaries, drivers, security guards, cooks, cleaners, gardeners and a constellation of other skilled and unskilled help. A key actor in this group is the facilitator who serves as the interface between the international partner and the government or local administration. The success of international humanitarian projects depends on managing the delicate relationship between the two camps. There are also indirect opportunities for hotel and restaurant workers, nightclub owners, tailors, barbers and mechanics, among many other trades. These opportunities, however, also create new forms of stress and perceived vulnerability: people are worried what will happen when the humanitarian business collapses and they find themselves out of work. One of Eric's colleagues echoes a widespread concern: 'The money is coming in today but it will dry up one day. Our international partners will fly out of Goma with their dollars and euros and leave us with a handshake. Thanks to them we learned English and some computer skills, but that isn't going to put beans in our dishes when they go back to the comfort and safety of their home countries.'

Waiting for the eventual withdrawal of the humanitarian agencies, their workers enjoy a special status in the collective imagination of Goma's population. 'The dream of every new graduate is to get a foot in the door of the sector – preferably with a United Nations agency, if not an international NGO. If that doesn't pan out, the young jobseeker would settle for employment in a local NGO.' Humanitarian workers with responsible positions have achieved a level of prestige equivalent to that of the rich trader, business leader or high-ranking civil servant – what Eric refers to as the 'closed circle of people who have attained well-being'. Some of his colleagues have a condescending attitude towards those who have not made it into this circle, considering that 'they are spectators, not players in the Goma arena'. The ostensible signs of this success are a new car, a villa in a good neighbourhood and a salary at the end of the month that alleviates the problems of family and friends. 'Their prestige is even augmented by the fact that they rub elbows with expats – even though it is an open secret that these latter are loathed for their sometimes real, sometimes imagined hypocrisy, arrogance, promiscuity, insensitivity and stupidity.'

THREE FACETS OF AN ALTRUIST

'Life in Goma has made me the way I am,' says Eric, 'and has driven me to achieve three ambitions: earn a living, enjoy the respect of the community, and pursue my altruistic ideals.' At the professional level, he has always been busy in different jobs that have allowed him to provide for his family. His current job with a Canadian drilling company as account manager testifies to his exceptional ability to shift from one work environment to another and to juggle multiple tasks at the same time: he continues to do accounting work for his longstanding network of clients, for example. His wife's nursing job supplements his income, contributing to the household expenses. These relatively comfortable circumstances put some of his past experiences into perspective.

> My humanitarian field operations severely constricted my family life. They could last for days on end, sometimes in areas where epidemics raged. In addition to the risk of contagion, these missions also ended with periods of quarantine. In conflict areas my life was under threat because the armed groups didn't give a damn about the neutrality of our red cross. When I was younger I wasn't particularly worried about these risks, but with age and maturity, I look at them from another standpoint.

The metal gate that separates his house lot from the rough lava street is adorned with a message that reflects the Kyungu family's Christian devotion. Visitors are welcomed with 'My home and my family serve the Lord'. An example of his generosity – and of him putting this into practice – is his hospitality to Gedion, a young man to whom he provided room, board and school fees. 'We took care of Gedion for two years – he never knew his father and his mother is an alcoholic with no money, no job and no education. A friend of mine, who didn't have the means to take care of him, asked me to help – which we did willingly.' Fellow parishioners at the Catholic Saint Bernadette church of Himbi, where he is a guidance counsellor, testify to his community engagement. 'Eric is on good terms with everybody and knows lots of things – that's why he always finds work,' says Mama Germaine, a widow who he has helped.

Combining professional and community work, Eric is indeed a busy man, but instead of indulging in self-satisfaction with his lifestyle, which many people in Goma would be jealous of, he prides himself on being available when called upon. 'I wouldn't go back onto a battlefield as a volunteer to gather dead bodies like I once would. I've come to accept my limits.' He is, however, thinking about future steps to capitalise on his experience with humanitarian agencies and his knowledge of his social environment. 'I don't have any firm plans but I think I could serve as a useful interface between the two. Who knows? I may even start up a structure based on the SEPRONA model which first inspired my humanitarian spirit.'

CHAPTER 7

EVERYBODY LOVES BEANS

A MARKET FULL OF
LIFE AND DRAMA

Mrs Bernadette Mpunga is a complacent owner of a small wholesale depot selling Kivu beans in the local Alanine market in Goma's relatively bourgeois Himbi I district. Born and raised in Goma, she knows the city well and the different characteristics of its many markets – especially Alanine, where she has been a fixture for the past twenty years. The people of Goma love *mahalagi* (beans) and consider them a staple, so keeping up with demand keeps Bernadette busy. It is a competitive trade so she has to be clever in making sure she has the quantity and quality of beans to satisfy her customers. As her main challenge is keeping her depot well-stocked, she has to adapt to seasonal supply shifts, in addition to monitoring security problems in the Goma hinterland where she buys her *mahalagi*.

Most Congolese cities, large and small, have a main central market, such as Kinshasa's *Grand Marché* or Lubumbashi's *Marché de la Kenya*, where shoppers from even relatively distant neighbourhoods go to buy the ingredients for their meals, consumer items and other household products. These central markets are where the best deals and prices can be found. In Goma, however, there is no such market: every district has its own medium-sized market that caters to the shopping needs of local residents. Although rather laconic by nature, Bernadette can become quite the chatterbox when it comes to beans and markets.

> The Goma local markets have everything you need: new and used clothes, hardware stuff, fruits and vegetables, our famous Goma cheese, smoked, salted and fresh fish, *makala*, fresh meat and even live animals. From fancy stuff imported from Dubai to kitchen utensils – you name it, you'll find it. The markets in Virunga, Murara, Katoyi, Ndosho and Katindo all look a bit like Alanine: prices are comparable and the range of goods for sale is about the same. So someone from one neighbourhood wouldn't entertain the idea of going shopping in another. Even in the bustling area of Birere, where I grew up, there isn't a main central market. And Birere is a really busy place, with lots of wholesalers, where people from Goma, the outskirts and even our Rwandan neighbours come to fill their baskets.

Even though the different neighbourhood markets are not laid out exactly the same, there are a number of common traits. They have both covered and open-air sections. The municipality, together with local associations, usually takes the initiative in constructing the rudimentary covered parts of the market, which are little more than a roof on steel columns. A quick walk around reveals that goods are clustered in categories that may seem incoherent but are in fact understandable to the initiated shopper. Dried cassava tubers, for example, are not sold near cassava flour, which is sold next to corn or wheat flour. Local foodstuffs are usually laid out in the open-air sections and sold on the ground, placed on either tarpaulins or burlap bags or in plastic basins. Manufactured items such as tinned foods (tomato paste, sardines or corned beef, for example), soaps and cosmetics are presented on rickety wooden stands in the covered parts of the market. Higher-priced items such as costume jewellery, trinkets, electronic gadgets and batteries can be found in makeshift wooden display cases with chicken-wire doors.

It is not always easy to find one's way through the rows of these markets, and it takes some getting used to before being able to navigate from one end to the other. 'A newcomer sticks out like a sore thumb; I can see her from far way. But you can't blame her because there is no rhyme or reason to the way things are organised, and, of course, there are no written indications of where to find what,' says Bernadette. After a few visits, buyers and sellers get to know each other and the newcomers gradually get used to the layout. The smart shopper takes her time: 'I've seen young mothers in a rush who get confused and leave with potatoes in their basket instead of the sweet potatoes they came to get.'

The Alanine market is located on the south side of the road to Sake. A long building full of construction materials (cement, iron rods, nails, plumbing fixtures and electrical supplies) separates the road from the entrance to the market. It is obvious that there is a market nearby – especially between 6 am and 10 am – because of the swarms of bicycles, pushcarts and *tshukudus* heavily laden with bags of *makala*, cabbage, carrots and potatoes. Pungent smells are another telltale sign of the market and range from the stench of rotting cabbage and steaming animal excrement to the pleasant odour of spring onions. 'My depot is just a stone's throw away from the main entrance so I'm used to starting my work day with these smells that tickle my nostrils. They are part of my morning ritual and bring me good luck.' Bernadette combines business and pleasure at the market: 'My clients have become my friends and we always take the time to jibber-jabber about expenses, other people's business, family matters and our husbands. Everyone knows where to find me for a chat or to buy beans.'

One of the busier areas of Alanine is the one selling live animals and *makala* – in the open-air section. The sounds of cattle, goats, sheep, pigs and chickens converge in a cacophony that drowns out people's conversations. Neither the sound nor the stink seems to bother anyone. At the sight of a potential buyer, the animal sellers, who are always on the alert, scramble to be the first contact. Once contact is made, the seller takes the potential buyer by the hand with a friendly but firm grip, praising the attributes of the animal that is going to wind up on a grill or in a pot. At this point, talk gets serious. 'How much?

Are you crazy? I'll pay half that.' Although barter is indeed part of market life, there is no backtracking once a price is agreed upon; that would be considered poor market etiquette. Further on, in another part of the market, among the bags of *makala*, men covered in black soot give the impression of arguing because of their loud speech and wild gesticulations. They are attentive, however, to the arrival of a buyer and also scramble to be the first to offer their charcoal.

Bernadette holds the conviction that market shopping is an art form and that the purchase of different articles requires attention to specific details.

> If you want leafy greens like *sombe* [cassava leaves], *lenga-lenga* [amaranth leaves], *mutshitsha* [squash leaves] or *bishogoro* [young bean leaves], you have to be here early to buy directly from the producer and not a trader. The evening, on the other hand, is better if you are looking for fresh meat or fish because, as we don't have refrigerators, you can get some good bargains. Amongst us bean wholesalers, there is little competition. I respect the relationships between my sister sellers and their clients as they do mine. Of course, when a newcomer shows up, it's every woman for herself – we all do whatever we can to nail a sale.

To reel in a new customer, Mama Bernadette deploys a good dose of psychology, calculated according to the attitude and demeanour of the person. Sometimes she can be pushy, giving the impression that she is doing the buyer a favour by selling to her; in other instances she can play the role of a pitiable market woman who needs to make a sale. When Bernadette's colleagues play the same game, the cleverest one tends to win. But there are rarely any hard feelings between them. Bernadette even emphasises the strong sense of solidarity and respect. 'When one of us has to leave our spot and a regular client comes by, we wouldn't think of trying to sell to her. In fact, we sell for our sisters from their supply and turn over the money when she comes back.' Good faith is also expressed when one of the women runs out of beans; in that case, the others lend her beans so that she can keep her customers supplied.

MAMA BETTY

Bernadette Mpunga – Betty to her friends – proudly claims to be a real *Gomatracienne*. Her father, Jonas, is Nyanga and her mother, Rachel, is half Tutsi. The couple met in Rachel's mother's restaurant, where Jonas, who was then a stock boy in a shop, used to have lunch. Lunch was his initial reason to go there, but the prospect of seeing Rachel became as important. Rachel also looked forward to his lunchtime break and the two quickly started talking about things other than the menu. One thing led to another and Jonas declared his passion; Rachel acquiesced and shortly afterwards found herself pregnant. They married and rented a house in Birere with Rachel's mother's help. Bernadette, who was born in July 1977, grew up in the busy streets of Birere. She did not spend much time in school: while still a young woman, she opened up her own restaurant with the help of her parents, specialising in all kinds of bean dishes.

'I used to tag along with my mother when she did the shopping for her restaurant, so I easily got to know about the different kinds of beans for sale. She taught me how to bargain and eventually sent me off by myself to pick things up at the market.' As the first girl of the family, Bernadette was trained at a young age to assume domestic chores such as cooking, cleaning, shopping and looking after her younger siblings. Familiarity with this environment – and lack of other opportunities – is what led Bernadette to eventually make beans her livelihood. In addition to being a good little mama's helper, Bernadette blossomed in adolescence.

I had to learn to defend myself from my teachers when I was still in primary school. They liked me and gave me good marks but I know that I didn't deserve them: I wasn't that smart in reading and writing. When I was sixteen, my gym suit got me into trouble. One day, my gym teacher couldn't keep his eyes off me – and not only his eyes. He was big and strong and I was naïve. So guess what? I got knocked up. My parents were furious! To avoid problems with the law, Georges married me. I couldn't stay in school but was reassured by the idea of sharing my life with him.

Georges does not hide the fact that he was 'subjugated' by Betty's body – her smile, too – and admits having taken advantage of the teacher–pupil relationship. Neither of them, however, seems to regret their destiny and Georges continues to repeat how proud he is of his wife. By seventeen, Bernadette was both wife and mother. 'I was already used to domestic responsibilities so taking care of Georges came easy. Having a wedding ring to show off made things easier too.' But as the salary of a gym teacher was not enough to live on, Bernadette had to find work if they were to make ends meet. Her mother was sympathetic to the young couple's needs and convinced Jonas to lend their daughter $100 – just enough cash for her to start up in the bean-selling business. Her mother also agreed to take care of Junior so that Bernadette could focus on her buying and selling. 'My little man was better off with his grandmother in her restaurant than at the dusty market with me.'

Bernadette worked hard to earn herself a reputation in the bean business, motivated by the drive to make her household a success. She started her day early in order to get breakfast ready and take care of Junior. By 7.30 am she was already at her mother's house to drop off Junior and then hurried to Kasoko (a small corner market near the Rutshuru roundabout) where she had her stand.

The fact that my mother agreed to take care of my son was a huge help because it would have been hard to combine my two responsibilities. In the beginning,

I'd buy just one basin of *pigeon vert* (the kind of beans people prefer in Goma because they cook quickly) and sell them at a price slightly lower than what other sellers asked. In around two hours, I'd unload the full basin and then go buy another one. I averaged three such operations per day, and before heading home I'd deposit my earnings at the local savings and credit association (COOPEC). Everyone in the Rutshuru roundabout area knew me so I was able to earn some decent money – sometimes up to $20 a day. So paying 50 francs to the authorities to keep them off my back wasn't a problem.

Georges and Bernadette decided to use contraception 'to avoid the surprise of another pregnancy' because Bernadette was determined to give her business her undivided attention. 'My days at Kasoko were repetitive but peaceful.' At nightfall, she would meet Georges at her mother's restaurant and head home with Junior. She was stubborn about not wanting Georges to eat dinner at her mother's because she wanted to pamper him with her own dishes. 'I flatter myself at being a real cordon bleu. There's never a family gathering when I'm not involved in the kitchen.'

After a year of diligent work, Bernadette had put away $600. With Georges' consent she paid back her parents' loan. They were happy to prove that their business was solid and to be able to express their gratitude for the confidence Jonas and Rachel had in them. 'Even within the family circle, the question of honouring a debt is important. There are plenty of deadbeats in Goma and once you have that reputation, no one will lend you money. There is no shame in having cashflow problems – anyone may need a loan at some point.'

Bernadette had plenty of opportunity to observe the ins and outs of the wholesale business. She kept her eyes open and asked lots of questions. 'Where do you get your supplies? What about transportation? Do you know anyone in that village? Is there anything else I'd need to know if I wanted to get involved in wholesale trade?' Thanks to her experience in her mother's restaurant, she already knew a lot about the different qualities of bean (such as taste and texture), varieties and cooking techniques. 'I was pretty well ready to move into the wholesale trade but decided to persevere for another year in retail to put extra money away.' Bernadette and Georges calculated that they would need to have enough money to keep a stock of twenty full bags. The thing they wanted to avoid most was establishing a clientele and then running out of stock. 'If you disappoint clients once, they may not come back.' They did the maths and figured out that they would need around $2,500 to buy the beans, put a down payment on a depot in a good market and cover administrative fees. 'It was a lot of money for us but it was the investment we needed if we were to try to improve our lot in life.'

Georges wanted to help his wife in her business ambition. He contributed by getting information from his students whose families lived in the villages outside Goma about bean production and trade. During the summer school holiday of 1996, he visited dozens of villages within a 100 kilometre radius of Goma, scouting out Sake, Kirotche, Masisi, Ishasha, Rutshuru, Kanyabayonga and Kayna. The excursions were risky because of the massive influx of refugees and widespread insecurity in the early years after the Rwandan genocide. 'But my students from all of these different places served as guides, company and protectors.' From all the places visited, Georges would take bean samples back to Bernadette, who was becoming quite the expert in all matters *mahalagi*.

BEANS ARE MONEY

Bernadette and Georges realised that they would need to work as a team to optimise their chances of success. The prospecting of villages was already a solid contribution on Georges' part, and it gave him the motivation to assume complete responsibility for the supply side of the business. Bernadette could therefore devote all her time and effort to sales. Their business partnership was facilitated by a serendipitous event: Georges won $2,000 in a lottery organised by the municipality. 'It was truly a benediction for us, proof that the Lord Almighty was on our side.' Thanks to that windfall and Bernadette's savings, they were able to move ahead with their dream.

Bernadette had started looking into different market areas for their depot and decided on Alanine for three different reasons. 'Alanine is in a pretty classy district where people buy in decent quantities without asking for credit; it is close to a main road, which means that unloading supplies from the hinterland is easy; and there is no other big *mahalagi* depot there, so I would have a near monopoly in the wholesale business.'

With Georges at her side, Bernadette led the negotiations to obtain a 30 square metre depot at the eastern side entrance to the market. The owner is a local territorial administrator familiar with administrative procedures. It was large enough to stock 100 bags of beans – which exceeded their needs. The rent was $30 per month with an up-front six-month rental deposit of $180 required. The weekend after the agreement was reached, Georges and Betty went to Sake (23 kilometres from Goma) to purchase their first big order. Georges had already been there on reconnaissance but Bernadette wanted to be there to help him get the best deals and to make sure that he was able to verify the quality of the precious beans. They left early in the morning so that she would have enough time to show him the ropes. 'Once you see something that looks good, ask the price and then pretend to walk away. That's the way to start negotiating downwards – pointing out real or imaginary defects like size or moisture.' Bernadette spent the morning talking beans with the growers while Georges looked on. They bought a dozen 100 kilo bags of beans and rented a Fuso pickup to get them to the depot. Georges stayed on two extra days in Sake to buy another thirty bags – facilitated by his student network. He was looking forward to a warm welcome from Bernadette, whom he was sure would appreciate his purchases. She was indeed pleased and had good news herself: she had already sold the full lot of the twelve bags she had brought back just a few days earlier, so Georges' return came just in time. 'Maybe it was beginners' luck but I was convinced that we were on the right track. We turned beans into money. The future didn't look bleak, especially because I could tell I was good at getting customers.'

Georges, however, found the setting-up phase exhausting, and thinks it was a success mainly thanks to Bernadette's personality. He looks back on that period with fond memories.

I became a good *mahalagi* buyer more by luck than anything else. Monday through Friday I went to school to work as a gym teacher and spent the weekends in the Goma hinterland buying beans. I became quite familiar with the agricultural villages in the area and figured out where to get what variety of bean. I'd go to Rugare and Kirotche for *pigeons verts*, to the zone between Kanyabayonga and Kayna for *bulangeti*, Sake for little black beans, and to Bweremana for striped *mazembe*. Sometimes I would even provide seeds to farmers who would grow for me – this wasn't a problem because three months after delivering seeds, I could already go pick up the harvest. After a while people got to know me and if I didn't pay a visit for a while, my farmer friends would get worried and pretend to be angry with me.

Bernadette's clientele is comprised primarily of market women who have their stands near her depot. Those who buy exclusively from her get special treatment. They can leave their unsold beans in her depot (which is locked at night) and Bernadette lets them pay in instalments or extends credit to them if they really need it. 'I earn a decent livelihood thanks to these women so it's normal that I do them favours.' Restaurant owners – like her mother – constitute the second main category of buyers for her. Personalising relations is a business strategy for Bernadette, so, to keep restaurant buyers satisfied, after an order has been placed by mobile phone, she makes the delivery herself. They can buy on credit too.

> I caught on quickly that offering beans today for money tomorrow was the best way to maintain a group of return customers. And they spread the word to their friends, family members and neighbours. Because of these good relations, people from well beyond Alanine and Himbi come to buy their beans from me. Keeping up with supplies is a bit stressful but Georges has been able to keep up his end of the bargain. Believe it or not, working together as a couple has reinforced our marriage.

There is, nevertheless, some conjugal turbulence. Even though Bernadette has nagged Georges to give up teaching and do more to participate in their business, he is not so inclined. He likes his work as a gym teacher. Bernadette's fear is that he will fall under the spell of another young student and her own situation will be repeated. When the topic comes up, Georges does what he can to reassure her: 'Yes, dear, you stole my heart but that can never happen again with anyone else.'

They both recognise that their ongoing success in business is related to the way they divide up the work: 'Our progress has been slow but steady.' Since they started ten years ago, they have been able to expand their stock considerably: from a start of forty bags, they now have 100 in their depot. But success in business can have its downsides, according to Georges, who likes to keep a low profile: 'As soon as people see that you have it easy they become jealous, their eyes glitter with envy and that can bring on bad luck. We have never been robbed or attacked – thank God – perhaps because we don't show off.' Even though they are frugal by nature, as they have only one child, they do not feel compelled to scrimp and sacrifice. 'We live in a comfortable house, we both have decent wardrobes and we are able to put plenty of food on the table.' Everyone in Bernadette's family and his own have heard him repeat that often enough.

Comfortable at least for the time being – 'You never know what's down the road' – Georges and Bernadette are far from well-to-do. They are still renters, 'without a house of our own', living in Murara, a neighbourhood populated largely by people struggling to survive – which is not nearly as nice as Himbi I, where they have their depot. During the first ten years of their marriage they deliberately avoided having more children because

Bernadette wanted to focus on work. But today, she regrets that choice of lifestyle. After that busy period, they did try to have more children, but for 'unexplained reasons' she had a series of miscarriages. 'I'm sad about having only one child. We sacrificed not having more just for the sake of earning money.' But Georges does not seem to mind because at least their only son is doing well: 'Jonas Junior is studying agronomy at the University of Goma and has a promising future ahead of him. I'm sure he will be able to expand our bean business. We are planning to buy a farm for him where he can grow beans and where I can grow old.' But Bernadette has not abandoned hope of having another child: 'I've tried unsuccessfully getting help from doctors; now I'm counting on God.'

In the meantime, they work and save to fulfil their plans for the future. 'We were able to save enough money to buy a plot of land in the Katindo neighbourhood where we are going to build our own house. Once we do that, we will buy a farm outside the city where we can grow our own beans and become our own suppliers – with Jonas Junior's help.' Georges has opened negotiations with the traditional chief of Jomba, who still has community land management rights for two hectares of land. 'I'd much rather leave Jonas Junior a plot of land than a few physical education booklets.'

Georges is well aware of the physical risks involved in his excursions to the Goma outskirts to buy *mahalagi*: 'But so far, so good. I haven't had any major problems with rebels, militias or other negative forces because I'm careful about when and where I travel. The security situation changes from day to day here so one never knows.' These forays have given him the opportunity to make lots of friends and to learn about farming, which he has come to appreciate. 'Once I become a farmer myself, I'll be able to respect Bernadette's hope for me to give up teaching gym.'

BEANS ARE EVERYWHERE

The omnipresent black volcanic earth is covered by subsistence crops all over the city. The smallest strip of public and private land is cultivated with some kind of crop – but beans predominate. The colours of the city's ground are green and black. Georges and Bernadette talk about market gardening with such enthusiasm it is almost like they believe they invented it. They cannot help interrupting each other once they broach the subject. For the former, 'The natural fertility of our soil encourages just about everyone – rich and poor – to plant beans. That explains why everyone has beans on the table.' For the latter, 'The unemployed of Goma plant beans to survive. But they don't limit their farming space to the city itself; the peri-urban areas to the west and north of the city are farmed and crops even help feed our neighbours in Rwanda.'

The black ground may not look conducive to bean growing but that is a misperception, according to Georges. 'Our region may be cursed but the earth is blessed. The little bean sprouts pierce their way into the cracks of hardened lava and thrive thanks to the rich nutrients they find there.' Many of the fields in and around Goma are constituted of lava beds from eruptions of the Nyiragongo and Nyamuragira volcanoes.

Bean fields produce four different comestibles. *Bishogoro* are the tender green leaves that are ready to pick around a month after the bean plant has taken root. Slightly bitter, they are served with rice or *fufu*, a thick and sticky paste made from manioc flour. *Mikekenye* are young pods in which the beans are hardly formed and that look and taste like a combination of green beans and spring peas. *Musekwa* are fresh, fully grown beans that have not been dried. They are available for a short time just after harvest and should be eaten the day they are picked because they wilt quickly under the Kivu sun. *Musekwa* are commonly served with *bisamunyu* (boiled green bananas). Then, of course, there are the bean staples: *mahalagi*, beans dried in their pods on the vines. It takes around two hours to boil *mahalagi* in one pot while different combinations of onions, garlic, celery, leek and nutmeg are frying in another pan. The people of Goma prefer these recently dried beans because if they are conserved for more than a couple of months they require special handling. They are then called *nyamukuru*. Having grown up as a restaurant woman's daughter, Bernadette has strong opinions about these products and loves to share them.

Nyamukuru are delicious if you know how to prepare them – and if you have plenty of *makala*. The slower the cooking time, the better. Start with plenty of water to avoid having to add – on a low heat you can control the evaporation speed. After cooking all afternoon, there shouldn't be any water left and the beans should be soft but not mushy. Seasoned with fresh leeks, onions and chives – ingredients that most people can afford – this *nyamukuru* preparation served with potatoes or sweet potatoes is a real feast. *Bishogoro* (up north they call them *musoma*) have to be picked early morning while the dew is still on them. That way they stay nice and fresh. You wash them in clean water and then simmer them for not more than fifteen minutes. Put your salt in before they start to simmer. In another pan start heating up oil while they are draining in a colander. Add spices to the oil and then fold in the greens with some peanut butter. Some women add smoked or salted fish in the final simmering phase.

Just about everyone in Goma eats beans, and in some families they are part of at least one – maybe two – of the daily meals. A family gathering without beans is inconceivable. Families that can afford to, buy a full 100 kilo bag at a time, at a cost of between $50 and $60 depending on the season. Others buy their beans on a daily basis at the market where a standard unit of measure of around 1 kilo (a *murongo*) costs approximately a dollar, again depending on the variety and time of year.

The Kivu bean, in Georges' opinion, is a 'strategic product not unlike conflict minerals because everyone wants them'. Goma and the region supply beans to

Rwanda, Uganda and elsewhere in East Africa, which increases prices for the locals. Georges' comparison seems exaggerated but reflects real problems about access to farmland in the densely populated Goma hinterland. For the DRC market, Kivu beans are transported by lorry to Kisangani, from where some are sent downriver by barge to Kinshasa. In the capital's market, the label '*madesu ya Goma*' (*madesu* is the Lingala word for bean) is well-respected: 'People prefer them to varieties from Bas-Congo or the Kasais.' Before the road from Butembo to Kisangani was refurbished, sacks of Kivu beans were sent to Kinshasa by air.

'From a humble little business we have been able to find serenity for ourselves.' Bernadette claims to have found fulfilment in her vocation and to be satisfied with the way she has organised her business and family life. 'I'm sensitive to the fact that being the main earner in the couple could put Georges ill at ease but we have both come to terms with that situation.' Both say that they consider themselves useful to the population by contributing their efforts and imagination to getting beans from field to cooking pot. According to Bernadette, beans – and mealtimes in general – 'are one of the few pleasures we have left in Goma where damnation and misfortune can strike you down when you least expect it'.

CHAPTER 8

THE MOTORBIKE
TAXI SOLUTION

NEW TRANSPORT NEEDS
FOR A SPRAWLING CITY

Motorbikes are everywhere in Goma. The revving of their motors – along with the first cock-a-doodle-doos of the roosters – are the wake-up calls that gradually invade the city. Shortly after dawn, motorbike taxis are criss-crossing every Goma neighbourhood in their hundreds, noisy, raising dust, looking for a fare. Swerving in and out of traffic, the motorbike taxi driver seems oblivious to the danger he runs for himself and his passenger. The beeping of their horns has become such a familiar sound that no one pays attention to it. This morning spectacle is one of the idiosyncratic experiences of a new day in this busy city. The municipality undertook an effort to establish the number of motorbikes and announced an approximate figure of 40,000. Given that Goma has a population of one million, that translates as one motorbike for every thirty inhabitants, which would be the densest concentration in any Congolese city.

The collective use of the motorbike came gradually to Goma in the late colonial period. At first, it was adopted as a private means of transportation by middle-class folk who could afford something better than a bicycle but couldn't purchase and maintain a car. Goma's bumpy, rocky streets were hardly conducive to automobile use, which remained confined to the colonial city area. Thanks to its speed and adaptability, the motorbike was to become the logical transportation solution.

Missionaries and administrative agents were the first to use motorbikes in the region. These were Japanese Yamahas, Kawasakis, Hondas and Suzukis. Their use as taxis emerged in the early 1990s and can be explained by the need for people to get around, but more importantly because of the relative affordability of Indian and Chinese imports. Reluctant at first, the city's population has come to accept the risk of falls, dust and collisions. The Chinese-made Boxer TVS – which costs around $1,000 – is the common make plying the streets of Goma and the dirt tracks of its outskirts.

In 1988, the Greater Kivu province was subdivided into three new provinces: North Kivu, South Kivu and Maniema. This reorganisation had major demographic, administrative and commercial repercussions for Goma, which became the provincial capital. New civil servants arrived and new businesses were established, creating needs and opportunities for a city that was expanding spatially while becoming increasingly cosmopolitan. Socio-economic change necessarily brought about new transportation needs – to commute between home and place of work, for example. The poor continued to walk but the emerging middle-class acquired bicycles, motor-cycles and automobiles. After the volcanic eruption of 2002, the city had only a few kilometres of asphalted roads in the commercial downtown area, but roadworks have moved ahead significantly in the past few years, funded by international partners. Roads in the residential neigh-bourhoods are neglected: 'a headache for car owners but a benediction for tyre merchants and mechanics'.

FROM SLOW LEARNER TO FAST DRIVER

The motorbike taxi profession is reserved for men like Papa Asumani Birewa, who has years of experience 'inhaling dust' on Goma's roads.

> I was forced to quit school at fifteen when my father died. I was a slow learner so the family wasn't willing to pay my school fees. I got a job as a clerk in my home village of Bweremana in Masisi, 45 kilometres from Goma. When my older brother Leonard got an admin-istrative job and moved to Goma, where he could enjoy the privileges of modernity, I followed. That was 1990. He tried to get me a job in an office too but months passed without an offer.

Asumani was thirty-one when he moved to Goma, where he lived with Leonard. 'I didn't realise it at the time but the fact that my brother had his own Yamaha changed my life. He used it to get back and forth to work and to visit friends but didn't care about earning money with it. There were not many taxi motorbikes at the time.' Asumani, who already loved bicycles, says he became obsessed with motorbikes. 'I wasn't working so had plenty of free time. I'd hang out with mechanics to learn everything I could from them. They are the ones who urged me to become a taxi man.' Leonard, however, was going to need some convincing before letting his brother use his motorbike as a taxi.

'It's not complicated, but to survive as a driver in Goma you need two assets in addition to being a good mechanic. You have to be physically strong, with enough weight to avoid being thrown off your bike. The roads are so bumpy it is easy to find yourself in a ditch – especially if you take your eyes off the road even for a second.' Short and stocky, Asumani did weightlifting to prepare for the conversation with Leonard. The second requirement is 'printing the map of Goma in your brain'. For this, Asumani devoted a couple of months to walking all over the city to learn 'every street, alley and cul-de-sac'. Satisfied with his preparations, he asked Leonard for approval. 'Big brother readily agreed and even helped me get a licence and insurance.'

Asumani started using his brother's Yamaha as a taxi a few weeks shy of his thirty-second birthday. 'I was still carefree, wasteful and satisfied to live day to day in that phase of my life. I wasn't married then, no one depended on me, so I didn't worry about saving money.' At 7.30 am he would drive Leonard to the provincial division of the interior where he had his office and then start picking up rides until around 10 am, when traffic slowed down. At lunchtime, traffic picked up again, and it was steady all afternoon. Asumani was busy until it was time to fetch Leonard after work. They would stop at a bar to count the day's earnings – a good part of which was immediately spent on beer. The rest was used to fill the petrol tank for the next day. This phase lasted for a few months. 'I lived under Leonard's roof and his wife fed me – I didn't need to think about tomorrow. The motorbike was just something to do until big brother got me a real job in his office.' But Asumani eventually realised that he was not about to get such an opportunity, because Leonard did not have the necessary pull, especially for a brother without a diploma. 'My chances were zero. At that rate, I was going to be dependent on him forever – which might have happened if I hadn't met the Hunde girl who was to become my wife. Eugénie was twenty-one at the time. I woke up thanks to her. Renting my own place was the first step in my ambition to survive on my own.' It was in this context that Asumani was inspired to become a professional driver.

He needed to acquire his own motorbike to integrate fully with the social universe of the *taxi motard*. To do so, he joined a rotating credit and savings system organised by *motards*, contributing around $20 a week. 'This was a considerable amount of money at the time for someone like me with my limited earning capacity. But the sacrifice paid off because after six months I had enough money saved to buy my own motorbike: a Yamaha 125 TF. I returned Leonard's motorbike to him, expressing my very deep gratitude.'

I paid $800 for my Yamaha, which was in excellent condition. The former owner wanted to get rid of it because he bought it as an investment – to use as a taxi. But his *motard* was unreliable, inventing all kinds of police hassles and lying about fines he had to pay. It's true that the motorbike's papers were not in order and the driver didn't have a licence, but that wasn't my business. I wasn't worried about those problems because I was friends with the traffic police and my papers were in order. I was on the verge of being a real boss, without having to ask anyone anything.

Asumani's next ambition was to settle down with Eugénie, who was twenty-two at the time. 'It is considered shameful for a Hunde girl to live with a man without respecting our tradition so I had to pay her dowry before she could live with me.' Once her father accepted the dowry and the arrangements for the wedding were made, the couple rented a house in the Majengo neighbourhood, which they were able to furnish week by week with Asumani's earnings. 'I wasn't doing badly – around $30 a day that I didn't have to share with no boss.' An energetic driver like Asumani transports around twenty-five passengers per day with an average fare of between $1 and $2 depending on the distance. Petrol, oil, occasional spare parts and a few banknotes for the traffic police add up to between $10 and $15 a day. 'My $30 covered our expenses and allowed me to save around $200 every month.' After two years of saving he bought a lot in Murara for $800 and put their plank house up at a cost of $1,200. He also constructed a garage that served as a workshop and safe place to keep his growing fleet of motorbikes.

'I finally had my own place for the family.' Eugénie had a girl in their first year of marriage and a boy two years later. But she experienced complications during the second delivery, which put an end to her child-bearing aspirations. 'It was God's will so I accepted the situation. We are a happy family even though God gave us just two children,' says Eugénie, with a mix of resignation and frustration. Asumani is rather laconic when it comes to expressing his inner feelings but did relate an incident that took place when the children were still young. 'They would be in bed when I left in the morning and again in bed when I returned at night. We *motards* have to accept long hours to get ahead.' One day, his daughter saw him sitting at the table and asked her mother: 'Mama, who is that guy anyway?' After that, he decided to spend all day Sunday with wife and children.

Asumani continued to put money in the drivers' rotating credit system (*tontine*). 'I knew the tricks of the *tontine* and took advantage of it. There were financial benefits, but, more importantly, contacts with young drivers helped me too.'

I used my first motorbike for a year and then sold it for $800. It was in good condition because these bikes are designed well – if you respect them with regular mainte-nance, they respect you in return. I used that money plus savings and bought a brand new one for $1,500. Every year – or two years maximum – I was able to buy a new motorbike which I rented out to my young colleagues. I had ten at one point, which was just right to earn money, manage the drivers, take care of maintenance and avoid envious feelings from people who were less lucky than I.

Even though Asumani had a successful strategy of accu-mulation and management, he did not give up his work as a driver until late in life. 'My family responsibilities taught me to be frugal, so I was able to build a house of lava stone and cement stucco on my lot which we moved into, renting out the original one to tenants.' He claims to be satisfied with his relations with neighbours and, most importantly, with all the young drivers he trained. 'I have a paternal relationship with these boys, who respect my lifestyle. They are always asking me my opinion about decisions they need to make.' After more than twenty years of expe-rience, he has recently started to slow down. 'I don't feel like dealing with the bumps and dust and backaches that didn't bother me when I was younger. I continue at a relaxed pace now more out of habit than necessity.'

The worst part of the job is the risk of road accidents – and Asumani had two close calls: the first in 1996 and the second four years later.

I was going at breakneck speed along the airport road to buttonhole a colleague who owed me money. As I sped past a parked lorry, I came face to face with a woman who was crossing the street. It was impossible to avoid the collision: she suffered a broken tibia and I ended up in a ditch, badly scratched but with nothing broken. I was taken to the police station for questioning and the victim to hospital. Of course I had to pay all her bills. My friendly relations with the police were a benediction because they let me go. Otherwise the victim's family could have taken justice into their own hands. When the woman was out of danger, I contacted her to arrange for compensation. I had to sell one of my motorbikes and buy her a house lot worth $500.

The second accident happened at night when Asumani was driving an officer to Sake, where his unit was stationed. Soldiers had set up a control post made of lava blocks at the city limits, which Asumani did not see because his headlight was defective. They crashed into the lava blocks, throwing both driver and passenger into space. His client was not hurt but Asumani received a serious head injury that landed him in hospital for three weeks. 'The officer was a kind soul: not only was he not angry but he even paid my medical bills. I had to rest another two weeks at home but then I was back on the road with the same motorbike.' These accidents taught him to be as cautious as possible – 'a lesson I repeat to my young colleagues'.

The Kivus are known and respected for the dynamism of their trade associations – and the motorbike sector is part of this system, with its Association of Motorbike Drivers (COTAM) and the Association of Motorbike Owners (COPTAM). Joining is voluntary, but once the entrance fee of $50 is paid, membership is for life. Both associations help their members with their papers: licence, insurance, and road tax authorisations. They also play a credit and savings role. Members also lend support to each other and families in cases of accident or death. Asumani took advantage of some of these benefits when he was getting established in the business, but eventually he distanced himself from them due to disillusionment. 'I know that there is strength in numbers but I realised that our fees were poorly managed and the associations were not particularly efficient in helping us get our papers. My main concern was the director or treasurer simply disappearing with our money.'

A DAY IN THE LIFE
OF A *MOTARD*

'Hey! Where are you going? Come on! I'll take you there.' That is the way that Asumani, like other *motards*, greets his potential passengers. 'Competition can be tough so you have to be alert. As soon as you see someone who may be looking for a ride, you rush up and start discussing the fare before your rivals intervene. You have to have the right feeling with a passenger because you need to earn a decent fare but you have to be reasonable. Minibuses, collective taxis and private taxis are other options for them.' Weather conditions influence which mode of transportation to adopt. If it is very hot or raining, people prefer these other taxis. Cost is also a factor: a ride that costs $2 with a *motard* is around 50 cents in a collective taxi.

Different factors influence the fare charged: the appearance of the potential passenger, the distance and the time of day. Passengers are usually careful to establish the price before getting on the motorbike to avoid any arguments upon arrival at their destination. The *motard* takes advantage of these situations by trying to squeeze a few extra francs out of the naïve client. If the *motard* is intransigent or if the passenger does not have enough money, a litany of mutual insults follows – in some cases ending in a fight. In the event of such confrontations, passers-by get involved but usually take sides with the passenger. 'Despite the fact that we *motards* provide a great service to the population, we are still considered as being greedy and unsavoury.' Asumani admits that some of his brother *motards* do in fact do whatever they can to take advantage of passengers. 'They didn't get good guidance at home so are ignorant of the values of honesty and good manners. They are more interested in looking cool and showing off to girls. This obviously requires money. Their greedy behaviour is a disservice to our brotherhood.'

Asumani gets out of bed at 5 am, wakes up the guard who spent the night in the garage and has him take out the motorbike he'll use that day. His drivers take it in turns to sleep in the garage – an important surveillance responsibility to avoid the bikes or tools being stolen. The other drivers arrive early and prepare their workday by inspecting the bikes: brakes, clutch cables, tyres, lights and fuel lines must be in order. Whatever repairs or adjustments are needed are done on the spot. 'When everything is ready, my boys exit the lot in the hope of having a safe and profitable day. When they hit the streets, they rev up their engines to let people know they are ready for service.' Bus drivers, who also need to start their days at dawn, are the first wave of passengers – many of whom reserved a driver the night before. Asumani jokes that his drivers 'are the early birds of the early birds'. The next wave is shopkeepers, lower-ranking civil servants who open public offices, security guards and women who have their makeshift stands selling coffee and doughnuts. 'By preparing the city for a new day, my *motards* are key actors in giving Goma its urban character.'

By 10 am, things start to slow down and the *motards* can relax and have breakfast. Asumani tells his boys to have fresh milk with their doughnuts but knows that some of them drink *sapilo* (a strong locally distilled alcohol). 'The job of a *motard* is physically exhausting so keeping fit is a priority. But this doesn't stop lots of them from using drugs [sniffing glue or petrol or smoking marijuana].' Asumani says that, instead of taking drugs, 'a couple of beers at the end of the day' are enough to keep him satisfied. Work picks up again in the afternoon when people break for lunch and head home or to a restaurant. Unlike in many other Congolese cities, where workers have an uninterrupted workday of shorter hours without a midday break, *Gomatraciens* are used to having a proper lunch. 'My *motards* are busy all afternoon with passengers doing shopping and administrative tasks and then, for others, heading home after work.'

Now that Asumani has decided to slow down, he devotes the afternoon to other activities. 'In this city where anything can happen for the worst in the blink of an eye, I got involved in some other business ventures – notably investing in my kids.' He helped his daughter set up a beauty salon where she also does sewing and he set up his son with a telephone boutique where he sells phone credit. 'The boy uses his earnings to cover his expenses at the University of Goma, where he studies agronomy.' At home, Mama Eugénie distils *kanyanga* (an alcohol made from maize and cassava), which she sells to a network of local distributors. 'After helping out the kids and Madame with their errands, I head into the garage and play around with my motorbikes – my favourite hobby – waiting for the boys to come back. When their days are done by around 8 o'clock in the evening, we clean the bikes, fill the tanks and secure the garage. Tomorrow will be another day.'

MOTORS OF SOCIAL CHANGE

The widespread use of the motorbike for the transportation of goods and people first started in Goma (facilitated by its proximity to East Africa) and then spread through the territory – even the population of Kinshasa, who were reluctant at first, have adopted it. The motorbike in Congo today is somewhat similar in terms of social change to the mobile phone twenty years ago, when it was a major innovation. Built in Chinese and Indian factories, motorbikes are sold at affordable prices and constitute a real boost in improving the well-being of ordinary people. Maintenance is relatively easy and they are well-adapted to urban streets and rural tracks – even during the rainy season, when in the past transportation came to a standstill.

In rural landscapes, the profitability of the motorbike is directly linked to the availability of mobile phones and mobile coverage. Food and charcoal producers communicate with *motards* and intermediary buyers who in turn organise transportation with lorry drivers. 'Everyone benefits. Thanks to communication and transportation, food doesn't rot in the fields or in village depots like it did in the past – and transporters don't have to wait weeks on end to fill their lorries with goods. The utility of the motorbike shuttling goods back and forth between village and urban market is now welcomed by everyone.' The image of a heavily laden bicycle pushed by an exhausted man is gradually disappearing, changing into one of a young man proudly straddling a motorbike with a bag of cassava, a yellow plastic jug of palm oil or even a pig or goat strapped on to the redesigned carrier rack. 'The days when it took forever to get a load from one place to another on a bicycle are past – the motorbike does all that in a day now.' Another example of this kind of change comes from the city of

Kisangani: its famous *toleka* bicycle taxis are increasingly rare, having been replaced by the motorbike.

As the purchasing power of the young villager or city dweller is weak, coming up with the approximately $1,000 to $1,200 to buy a 125cc motorcycle is beyond the reach of most. But young men covet them because they represent modernity, prestige and freedom. Many Congolese believe that the appearance of motorcycles is a witchcraft phenomenon – people enter into pacts with sorcerers to acquire them by sacrificing family members. Many of the motorbikes on Congo's rural tracks are purchased by traders who advance payment for them – in exchange for promises of agricultural goods. Young men consequently enter into a kind of servitude to pay off their debts. The motorbike's impact may be slight in terms of agricultural marketing, but it is an emerging positive trend whose ramifications are difficult to predict. While it is unlikely that the motorcycle will contribute significantly to feeding Congo's towns and cities from a macro-economic perspective, it is nevertheless already augmenting rural revenues. Asumani summarises these trends by saying that 'in towns and in villages, the motorbike provides an innovative solution to our transportation needs'.

DISCRETION MAKES A DIFFERENCE

'The *motard* always has money in his pocket, which isn't the case with the road police. That's why we are constantly taken advantage of. We have to keep up friendly relations and the police know that they can hassle us only to a certain extent. The motorbike is like the goose that lays the golden egg – no one wants to kill it.' In addition to handing over a few bills to the police at the city's main crossroads, Asumani adds that 'showing respect doesn't cost extra' – testifying to his sense of pragmatism. 'Relations with the police make the difference between a good day and a bad day for us.' The following conversation between Asumani and his colleague Lukale puts this comment into perspective.

It is 11 am, a quiet time for Goma's *motards*. Asumani and Lukale are having a break in front of their litre bottles of fresh milk, waiting to be served their snack of fatty chunks of pork. '*Yaya* [big brother], I have headaches with the police and need some advice. You have been around for as long as I can remember. Explain to me why I never see them giving you a hard time. I had a small accident the other day and that mean officer Musafiri fined me $50. I don't have that kind of money but if I can't propose something acceptable, he said he was going to confiscate my motorbike. Then what would I do? Can you talk to him for me?' Asumani replied curtly: 'You have these kinds of disagreements because you are proud and stubborn. What's the big deal in saying you're sorry, it won't happen again, and calling him *patron*. You end the apology with a handshake of a few hundred francs and he'll let you go about your business.'

In July 2013, municipal authorities banned *motards* from the streets after 6 pm unless they were wearing a numbered fluorescent vest purchased at the town hall. 'We had to comply with the rule, supposedly for security reasons. They argued that it was a way of limiting acts of violence and banditry. We knew that it was just another trick invented by the authorities and police to squeeze money out of us.' But the *motards* passively protested – not driving after dark. 'We spread the word not to buy the vests. After a while the population made it known to the authorities that they were the main victims and the ban was lifted in March 2014.'

CHAPTER 9

PRIVATE SECURITY
FOR HIRE

A SOLDIER OF
WAVERING ALLEGIANCE

The Warrior Security, K K Security, HDW-SD, Top-Sig, Delta, Eagle View, G4S, Kami HSS, Latlong International and Graben are just a few of the many private security companies in Goma that are involved in a fierce competition to exploit the market in protecting international humanitarian workers. Banks, companies and well-to-do Congolese are also part of their clientele. The sector emerged in the aftermath of the Rwandan genocide to fill the vacuum left by government forces unable to provide security. But not only have government forces not been able to provide security, it is also often alleged by reliable sources that they are in fact perpetrators of acts of violence against civilians, of pillaging, thievery and extortion. In this context, only those who can afford the services of private security companies have any hope of securing their belongings and personal safety. Private security professionals have thus become fixtures on the Goma landscape, where 'a Kalashnikov can be purchased for less than the price of a goat'.

Papy Bahati Assani is a 2-metre-tall giant who looks like he could be a professional basketball star. He was born to Bakumu parents on 16 January 1976 in Isiro in today's Haut-Uele province (formerly Maniema). He remembers his family being well-off: his father was director of a soap and cosmetics factory transforming palm oil, while his mother bought and sold women's clothing between Isiro and Bujumbura. His parents were generous and easy-going. 'Kids were jealous of me when I was a boy. When one of my classmates would say he was hungry, I'd bring him home and get him fed. I had never gone hungry and didn't comprehend how someone could not have food or money for food. But that was a bitter reality I was to learn the hard way just a few years ahead.'

His parents divorced in 1982 when Papy was just six years old and his father remarried immediately after-wards. His mother was more interested in her business than in her children, who came to expect neither affec-tion nor support from her. 'When she died three years after the divorce, I didn't shed a tear.' Shortly after the divorce and his father's remarriage, the family moved to Kisangani, where his father was transferred to manage his company's headquarters. They settled in the presti-gious Boyoma neighbourhood. Papy thought at the time that things would work out with his stepmother and his new environment, but he ruefully recalls that 'a good start doesn't get you to the finish line'.

The downward spiral started when his stepmother's first daughter was born. 'Not only did she neglect us but she did whatever she could to alienate us from our father by inventing all kinds of mischief that we were falsely accused of.' Papy and his siblings were consequently packed off to boarding school with the Marist Brothers of Kisangani. 'That's where I developed my love of sports – especially basketball and judo.' After boarding school, Papy attended the Nyangezi seminary school in South Kivu, where he graduated with his high school diploma in 1997. He then returned to Kisangani to be with his father, who had started looking into the possibility of sending him to university in the US. In the meantime, he attended classes at the seminary college of Kisangani.

In December 1997, Papy's father passed away suddenly. 'I lost all hope when Papa died. My life lost meaning; my plans were thrown into havoc, and the future – which looked good until then – was now bleak. To make matters worse, Sylvie, my white girlfriend who lived with her Belgian parents in the Boyoma neighbourhood, was pregnant.' To help him through his bereavement, Sylvie took him to Kinshasa to live. Papy experienced a brief twinkling of happiness when their daughter was born. 'Even though my mean stepmother succeeded in putting a wedge between my father and me, I adored him. After he went to his celestial reward I wasn't right. The only thing I could do to forget my woes was shoot hoops. Sylvie really didn't get it and criticised me for neglecting her and not paying enough attention to the girl.'

The beginning of the end of their love affair coincided with the disagreements between President Laurent-

Désiré Kabila and his Rwandan allies. When Kabila ordered Rwanda to leave the Congo, President Kagame fomented the second Congo war and set up a proxy in Goma – the Congolese Rally for Democracy (RCD). The Kinshasa population was outraged by Kagame's actions and cultivated a deep hatred for everything Rwandan. A manhunt ensued and real and suspected Rwandans were attacked. 'Plain-clothes policemen came to get me on the basketball court at the Place Commerciale of Limete where I used to shoot hoops. My height, which was great for playing basketball, turned into a near-fatal disadvantage. Someone probably told the police I was Rwandan – denunciation is a national sport in Congo.' Sylvie and Papy were not exactly on speaking terms at this point but were still living together. 'I didn't have anywhere else to go so stayed with her. I can't be sure, but I suspect Sylvie ratted on me to get me out of her life.'

All his efforts to prove that he was in fact Congolese and not Rwandan were in vain. 'I was sent to the horrible Makala prison and was savagely tortured for six months along with real Rwandan inmates.' An agreement was eventually reached between Kinshasa and Kigali for an exchange of prisoners and he was transferred to the Kanombe military camp in Rwanda. 'I was alone there with no friends and no family, but unlike the Congolese authorities, the Rwandans believed that I wasn't one of them and allowed me to be repatriated to Goma.'

Papy reunited with a paternal uncle upon his arrival in Goma in 2000 but was not made welcome under his roof, so quickly needed to make other arrangements. Thanks to the help of the infamous Laurent Nkunda, whom he had met during his deportation to Rwanda, he was able to get a seat on a military plane for Kisangani. His idea was to get his share of his father's estate, but that did not come to pass. 'Of course I didn't get anything. My stepmother had made her own arrangements by corrupting my father's lawyer. I was so disoriented I wanted to die. That's why I enlisted with the RCD.' Between 2001 and 2003, Papy actively participated in the conflict in and around Kisangani and was rewarded with a lieutenant's rank. 'Despite the risks I took on the front lines, I survived.' In 2003, a local radio station broadcast anti-Rwandan resistance messages, which caused a popular uprising. This hunt for Rwandans resulted in six casualties – the vigilante sentence was death by burning. The reprisals by the Rwandans were devastating.

Rwandan soldiers organised raids throughout the city. Civilians were taken to the bridge over the Tshopo River to be slaughtered. Five people were murdered. I did what I could to save some of them even though by doing so I risked by own skin. I don't want to think what would have happened to me if I was caught as a traitor. With my rank as an officer, I was afraid I could someday be associated with the massacre, so, absolutely disgusted, I deserted. Destination: Goma in civilian clothes.

Papy the deserter was able to stay with his little sister Giselle while looking for work. He tried entering the national police force with an officer's rank but was unsuccessful. 'After having commanded men, I wasn't about to be a common police officer. I should have known I didn't have a chance because I didn't have a godfather and tribalism excludes anyone from responsible jobs here if you're not from North Kivu.' After six months of frustration, he made friends with a relative of an adviser to the Minister of Defence. Thanks to his facilitation, Papy enlisted in the national army and was stationed in Bukavu under the orders of Colonel Mutebusi, who was in charge of military intelligence.

> I was involved in some very shady work. Betrayal and risk of death were part of the deal because of the high economic stakes of the region. I earned plenty of money and spent it freely. That's when I bought myself a Toyota Hilux. I was young and carefree and knew I could die anytime. My comrades were as reckless as they were unscrupulous. We received bonuses at the end of every operation – sometimes as much as $5,000.

This chapter in his life came to an abrupt end in June 2004 when Colonel Mutebusi tried to seize Bukavu on behalf of Rwanda. A few weeks after the unsuccessful attempt, President Kabila signed a presidential decree banning all soldiers from the national army who had served under the traitor. 'I found myself amongst a group of soldiers wanted for high treason so had to flee – leaving all my possessions behind. Destination: Goma as a fugitive.'

DOWN-AND-OUT

Papy found no trace of Giselle upon his return to Goma so had no place to stay. He spent a few nights on the street but by chance met up with an old classmate from the Nyangezi seminary school, Jacques, who invited him to stay with him and his mother. Within a few days, however, rumours started to spread about a very tall suspicious-looking stranger who had moved into the neighbourhood. People tend to know their neighbours in Goma – where all strangers are perceived as potential infiltrators and enemies. 'The city has experienced so many attacks, you can't blame them.' Newcomers stick out and people want to know who they are, where they come from and what they are doing. The first set of questions is addressed to the head of the household where the newcomer is staying, and concern their ties. If there are doubts about the person, the neighbourhood authorities are informed. Neighbourhoods are policed by neighbourhood chiefs who are seconded by street chiefs. If a street chief hears about anything suspicious, he investigates and reports to the hierarchy. The people of Goma are therefore reluctant to offer lodgings to potentially suspicious strangers for fear of getting into trouble and having to pay fines. This social control explains why Jacques' mother received orders from the neighbourhood chief to get Papy to leave.

'When I said goodbye to my friend Jacques I had only the clothes on my back and nothing in my pocket – and obviously nowhere to go. I would have gone hungry that day were it not for a wake where I spent the night. The mourners gave me a cup of coffee and a chunk of bread around midnight. Unfortunately, that situation didn't repeat itself.' It is common practice in Goma for mourners to welcome anyone willing to express their condolences. During the following weeks, Papy asked for charity and on some days met up with someone who would be willing to share some food and offer him a place to wash. Late at night he would ask bar owners if he could sleep on their plastic chairs. Sometimes he found a Good Samaritan but most nights he slept on the street, famished. 'My boyhood memories of helping my hungry classmates haunted me. I considered myself lucky when I found some menial tasks to do so I could buy food. Destiny was so unkind to me.' His life on the street lasted three months and then he met up with an evangelical preacher he had known in Kisangani who had tried to mediate on behalf of Papy and his siblings with their stepmother over their father's estate.

Preacher Kisirani lived in an apartment in Birere owned by a military officer. 'Religion has helped the people of Goma get through many problems and we listen to preachers who deliver messages of hope. Papa Kisirani just decided to help me – and get me off the street.' People from the neighbourhood were not suspicious this time. 'A Lord's servant commands trust and no one wants to mess with an officer.' Kisirani, however, was also unemployed and without any money – his generosity was limited to offering shelter. 'A roof over my head and a place to bathe and wash my clothes was a big leap forward after having lived as a homeless man.'

Papy's experience in Goma taught him a few things that provided him with work. 'I'd linger around the markets and bus stations looking out for people who needed help in finding their way in the commercial areas or help in carrying their purchases. My size and athletic look inspired confidence. They were willing to shell out a few dollars to avoid being robbed or tricked by the many crooks looking for prey.' Papy also befriended some bus drivers who would let him drive when traffic was light: 'It wasn't much money but at least enough to buy food.'

Preacher Kisirani was hired by an international NGO to help refugees three months after Papy met him. Life changed for the better for both of them then. Kisirani shared his money with Papy, who gradually found some serenity in his daily routine. He took his job search more seriously and even thought about going back to school. Nevertheless, 2004 and 2005 passed without his finding work other than the stewarding of shoppers and bus driving. 'My attitude changed, however, and I even rediscovered some of life's simple pleasures.' Indeed, Papy met a girl who boosted his confidence by showing affection: 'I hadn't been interested in a relationship with a woman after my problems with Sylvie – combined with my hard luck – but my new girlfriend opened my eyes and my heart.' Annie became pregnant almost immediately after their encounter and Papy went to see her parents to ask for her hand. Preacher Kisirani helped in the negotiations. Four months later – Papy had just turned thirty – he was authorised to live with his twenty-two-year-old fiancée, and shortly thereafter a daughter was born. 'It took a while to sink in but I finally felt I was becoming a responsible person. These were happy days for me. My mother wasn't affectionate and my father was reserved. Thanks to Annie and our daughter I discovered human tenderness.'

PAPY AT WARRIOR

After years of job seeking, Papy ultimately found work as a private security guard in 2006 with K K Security. He had to take psychological and physical exams before signing his contract and then undertake paramilitary training. 'As a family man I didn't have a choice and had to take what I could get. Earning a regular wage was a priority.' His first assignment was as night watchman in the Stella Matutina Hotel, along with two other men. The first lesson he had to learn was 'no sleeping on the job'. The guards would close the hotel's main gate at night, and while one man stood watch, the other two patrolled the compound. 'Our presence helped ward off petty thieves and our uniforms tended to reassure the mostly white guests.'

Despite a few minor differences in their organisation, most private security companies operate along the same lines. No private security guards are allowed to carry arms – which is a prerogative of the national army and the police. Rotating teams assure protection and are connected by walkie-talkies to a central dispatch head-quarters that sends out intervention units when a team is under attack. These intervention units may be accom-panied by armed police or soldiers who are mandated to open fire on attackers or thieves. Papy has not experienced many such interventions: 'Our main role is to be visible with our boots shined in front of a bank or company and greet the customers. The biggest danger we face is forget-ting to salute a boss or tarrying in opening the gate when he beeps the horn of his SUV.' According to Papy, private security guards have a somewhat better reputation in Goma than police or soldiers.

> We have neat uniforms and security equipment and people think our walkie-talkies are cool. When someone meets one of us at night on an isolated street, they do not have the fear they would have compared to meeting a soldier – who is often rightly perceived as being a brutal predator. Respect and good manners are part of our training. Even schoolchildren readily admit to their classmates that their father is a security guard, which they don't always do if he is a policeman or a soldier.

In addition to enjoying a decent reputation, Papy considers that the vocation offers other advantages as well. 'Most jobs require a six-day work week but we have two days off, which allows us to take care of other business and visit with friends and family. More importantly, our salaries are comparatively higher than those of most public workers, which explains why lots of police and soldiers leave their jobs to join a private company.' Papy suggests that private security companies recruit former soldiers because they are well-suited to fight against their former colleagues who engage in acts of banditry, pillage and theft: 'The best park rangers are former poachers!' He also points to a growing tendency to recruit female security guards, who serve primarily in banks and businesses.

The inhabitants of poor neighbourhoods who cannot pay for private security services are particularly vulnerable in Goma. 'Everyone is touchy about this security problem so local kids group together at night to stand guard. Armed with sticks and clubs (but not knives or machetes, which would get them in trouble with the police), they congregate at intersections and make fires to keep warm. To ward off sleep and cold, neighbours pitch in to buy coffee and sugar to show their appreciation.' In the event of a break-in, assault or mugging, people blow whistles or beat on kitchen pans to alert the self-styled vigilantes who come running. 'Their power is more in their numbers than in their skills. The presence of these groups can serve to keep petty criminals out of the neighbourhood, which is proof that if you help yourself, heaven will help you too.'

Papy has had some close calls in his work, such as the one he recalls below:

I was alone in a mineral depot owned by a local trader. It was 2 am and raining heavily – the rain dimmed the projector lights focused on hundreds of bags of cassiterite. The late hour and rain offered the right conditions for an attack. I heard a motor and then the slamming of doors announcing nocturnal visitors. I immediately left my observation tower and headed for the electrical circuit breaker while activating my mobile alarm [a handheld device that sends the alert to headquarters]. Monitoring the wall where I heard the vehicle stop, I saw two men climbing over it. I turned the lights off and made my attack. The intruders were surprised by the sudden darkness, which gave me the upper hand. I knew I was taking a personal risk, but as I saw that the men were not armed, I wrestled them to the ground and handcuffed them. Hearing the fight, the accomplice who had stayed outside starting shooting into the air. Pretending to not be alone, I screamed: 'Shoot! Shoot now! There is someone else outside. I already captured two of them.' The accomplice fell for the trick and drove off. The intervention team arrived a few minutes later, I switched the lights back on, and the two thieves were taken to the police station.

In recognition of this exploit – the theft of the minerals would have been a blow to the company's reputation – Papy was promoted to supervisor. 'I didn't have to stand guard or risk my life anymore and I got a good salary raise.' His new responsibilities consisted of training new recruits and dealing with the administrative planning of which guards should serve where. 'With my supervisor's salary I could refurnish the house, buy new clothes for Annie and my daughter and even put some money aside.' Papy, however, is an eternal malcontent and grumbler, and in 2008 he decided that his career in the company was not moving ahead as fast as he would have wished.

I was blocked in promotion possibilities for ethnic reasons and when I complained to the hierarchy – from North Kivu – they made it clear to me that I could either accept my position or make other arrangements. When my assistant got promoted to be my boss, I felt insulted, so I quit – slamming the door behind me. With my experience and good reputation, I thought I would get snatched up by another security company. That, however, was a stupid assumption. The agency bosses talk to each other and when someone quits or gets sacked, word gets around. They keep you hanging on with false promises but no offers.

Depressed and adrift, Papy fell back into a downward spiral. His savings dried up at the same time Annie had a second daughter. They started selling off their belongings to pay rent and buy food but the situation quickly got out of control. 'I didn't have the money to pay the rent and the landlord kicked us out.' Annie and the two girls went to live with her parents in their village and Papy stayed with friends. To earn a few francs, he resumed his old jobs as market guide and bus driver. 'For three long years I was unemployed and desperate. It took a long time to sink in but I finally realised that you don't throw away an old crutch until you have a new one.'

Papy's luck changed for the better in 2011 when a former director from K K Security, who had also quit around the same time Papy did, was contacted by an American security company that was setting up an agency in Goma to be named The Warrior Security. He asked Papy to work with him. 'The first few months were slow and I worked for free but we gradually established a clientele comprised of international NGOs, banks and some rich Congolese.' Word of mouth was in their favour, and, as their reputation became known, Papy started earning a salary: $50 per month at first and then $80. He was able to pay off the money he owed to his former landlord, find a new place to live and reunite with Annie and the girls.

At The Warrior Security, Papy worked his way up the ranks from patrol driver to supervisor, responsible for training and dispatching units to assignments. 'I'm one of the senior workers by now and get along well with the local team and with our American bosses who come to Goma once in a while. They send us lots of brochures in English which I have learned to read.' He is earning over $200 a month, which is enough to cover household expenses – but not enough to save. 'If I could earn at least $300 I'd be able to save and maybe even buy my own plot of land to build a house on – but I can't imagine that is ever going to happen.'

The difficult phase of unemployment, poverty and separation from his wife and daughters after he left K

K Security was a time of grand resolutions. 'First of all, I stopped smoking and drinking and then Annie and I turned to prayer. We are devoted to our evangelical church and the Bible has become my companion.' Since April 2012, they have lived in the compound of Annie's parents in Katoyi, at the request of her father who was transferred to Kananga. This was an opportunity for Annie and her mother to enter into a business partnership. In Goma, Annie buys North Kivu food (beans, onions, potatoes, cabbage and fresh meat) and manufactured products from East Africa and Asia (clothing, shoes and household electrical appliances) and sends them to Kananga, where her mother sells the stuff. 'The money Annie earns thanks to her mother's help is a useful contribution to our survival.'

SHARED VULNERABILITY

Papy Bahati draws a parallel between his own personal vulnerability and that of the city where he lives. He has adopted Goma and Goma adopted him. 'My destiny and Goma's have been like a crucifixion – defeat with no victory. War, humiliation, family betrayal, torture and xenophobia! What more evidence do you need? I've been forced to wander between Kisangani, Kinshasa, Kigali, Bukavu and Goma: these are all cities associated with suffering for me. For the time being Goma is home but that doesn't mean I'm happy here.' The security situation in and around Goma has improved, and at the same time Papy claims to have found at least a semblance of serenity. Nevertheless, as proof of the contradictions in his discourse, he says: 'We remain vulnerable and the future uncertain. I want to have hope but am afraid to hope for too much. My philosophy is to take every day at a time – carpe diem. In any event, it is good to have problems because, if you don't, it means you are already dead.'

Despite his tendency to brood and feel sorry for himself, his family responsibilities have made him more mature and tolerant. He has accepted his lot at The Warrior Security and does what he can to help Annie and her mother with their trade. 'I have the hope of going back to school one day, which is one reason why Annie and I have decided not to have more children.' Like so many other people in the DRC and elsewhere, hardship has inspired piety in Papy, who prays for safety and well-being. 'My uniform and security equipment are trivial. God is the only real shield against adversity.'

CHAPTER 10

GEMBLOUX–GOMA RETURN

AN AGRONOMIST WITHOUT BORDERS

Isabelle Michel, agronomist at the Katale Coffee Estate, first discovered Goma in 1981 as a tourist. Born and raised in Belgium, she never imagined at that first encounter that she would one day be part of the *Goma-tracien* family. But thanks to her agronomy degree and her love of coffee, it happened. And thanks also to her longstanding association with Goma and the Rutshuru region slightly to the north, she is well-placed to trace the evolution of the region as well as having the insight to be able to describe the challenges of carrying out a formal economic activity in a war zone. Isabelle expresses her real passion for coffee: 'We do the complete cycle of planting, producing, processing and exporting top-quality Arabica beans – and without any outside support, credit or subsidies. It's a huge commitment and responsibility. Coffee lovers have no idea of the investment involved in getting a quality brew into their cups.' Her story gives an idea of what that entails.

In 1981, a former classmate from Gembloux who was working for the Food and Agricultural Organization of the United Nations in North Kivu invited Isabelle and her husband Baudouin to visit Zaire – specifically Goma and the Virunga National Park. 'It was our first visit to this part of the world. Goma was a small town then – and it was peaceful. It was only many years later that I understood why our friend slept with a gun under his pillow. Himbi, the area where we rent our house today, was covered by forest.' Her initiation to eastern Zaire was unforgettable. 'We climbed to the Nyiragongo crater, slept in tents in the Virunga Park and saw lots of animals. I loved this exposure to nature. To get myself in the right frame of mind prior to our journey, I read Karen Blixen's famous book, *Out of Africa*. Our experiences were not exactly similar to hers but the discovery of the Kivus was absolutely magnificent.' The road between Goma and the park went through the Katale Estate – as it still does today. 'I was amazed by the neat alignment of the coffee bushes with their dark oval green leaves; but the idea of working there one day never entered my mind.'

Isabelle first lived in what was then Zaire in 1982 as a newlywed, when Baudouin was hired as an economic agronomist by an aristocratic Belgian family who owned the Kwilu-Ngongo sugar factory in the Bas-Zaire province. Both having recently graduated from the prestigious Gembloux agronomy institute (which is now part of Liège University), they moved to Bas-Zaire. As a child, Baudouin had heard lots of stories of the Belgian Congo from his parents, who met and married there in the 1950s. His mother was a social worker inspecting Congolese who aspired to the status of évolué (a kind of social accreditation in the colonial hierarchy) and his father was an officer in the army (*la Force Publique*). Isabelle was also familiar with Africans as a child because she had Rwandan bi-racial cousins, some of whom returned to live in Belgium after the 1994 genocide.

The young couple worked in Bas-Zaire and Kinshasa for ten years, returning to Belgium regularly to visit family and friends. 'We learned a lot about life and work in Zaire during those years, even though I found the neo-colonial mentality at the sugar factory oppressive and unsettling.' Isabelle's most treasured memories of the time were the years she worked with her close friend Gaby Castel. Together they managed the Joy of Learning bookshop on Kinshasa's Boulevard du 30 Juin between 1988 and 1990. Gaby confirms the pleasure of that initiative by recalling the story of a schoolteacher who bought a *Petit Robert* dictionary on instalment and would come every month to pay the debt little by little.

Those years were also fruitful from a family perspective: Sarah was born in 1984 (when Zaire was under World Bank control through structural adjustment programmes and President Mobutu won 99 per cent of the votes in the presidential election of June); Noa was born in 1989 (Mobutu lost his Western backing when the Berlin Wall collapsed in November); and Isabelle gave birth to their third daughter, Milena, in 1991 (a year of tense social relations and violence).

The political, economic and social context had become untenable in the late 1980s and President Mobutu himself was forced to admit that the Second Republic had failed. People were at the end of their tether. The military had been unpaid for months, and, joined by a severely impoverished populace, took to the streets in many of the country's major cities in September and October 1991 in a wave of looting and violence. The pillaging destroyed what had remained of the formal economy, industries and infrastructure. Kinshasa and Bas-Zaire were particularly hard hit. The Michel family returned to Belgium to wait for the situation to stabilise. A new opportunity to return to Zaire emerged before long. The Katale Coffee Estate was up for sale. Isabelle and Baudouin did not have the wherewithal to purchase the estate on their own, but they were able to convince the Damseaux – a Belgian family with longstanding investment experience in the country – to go into partnership. 'I was absolutely delighted because, other than my experience with Gaby, I didn't really love Kinshasa or the sugar factory environment.'

The idea of relocating to Kivu, however, was tempting. 'I felt good in Goma, mainly because of the inhabitants. They are friendly, serious and hard-working. Goma is a cosmopolitan city, and as the Swahili-speaking people are used to business travel, their views are broader than those of the Kinois.' Although she has picked up only a few words and expressions, Isabelle also emphasises the elegance of Swahili, which contrasts sharply with the aggressive sound of the Lingala spoken in the capital.

'Another advantage is Kivu's temperate climate and the beauty of its landscapes.'

From 1992 to 1996, the family shuttled between Goma – lodged in a quaint bungalow within the luxurious environment of the Karibu Hotel on the banks of Lake Kivu – and the plantation headquarters located 50 kilometres away. 'There was a beautiful house at the estate but we couldn't live there permanently. We had to be in Goma to be able to evacuate through Gisenyi in the event of security issues; plus, there wasn't a school there.' They put the girls in a school that followed the Belgian curriculum. 'A nice little school with around a hundred students.' Through work and school, the family established a diverse social network. Weekends and school holidays were spent at the estate and in the nearby parks (Virunga and Rwindi). 'Life was beautiful and carefree for us. There were hints of the problems that were to befall the region in the coming years but we were oblivious to them. Kivu can also be very unsettling.'

THE KATALE COFFEE ESTATE

The Katale Estate is the only officially registered coffee plantation in the DRC, located in the Rutshuru district. It employs approximately 2,000 workers depending on the season, who tend to over 1,000 hectares of coffee bushes that are neatly maintained along a 20 kilometre stretch of fertile land that borders the Virunga National Park. A team of five Congolese agronomists are in charge. 'They are amazingly committed and resourceful in the ways they manage the estate while dealing with the serious security challenges we have gone through since the genocide and refugee crisis.' Harvesting, which takes place twice a year, is done primarily by women. Men take care of the more technical and agricultural tasks of clearing, weeding and trimming the bushes. They are also involved in the preliminary phase of processing the beans through washing and drying, which includes pulping (removing the skins from the coffee fruit) and hulling (removing the green coffee bean from the parchment shell).

Annual production fluctuates from one year to the next – just as international prices do – but for the past few years it has been around 350 tonnes. The tropical climate, volcanic soil and high altitude are particularly conducive to high-quality taste and texture. 'Sun-dried, our beans are never bitter; they are ripe but not over-ripe. The smell is perfect and the taste is always rich and well-balanced.' The production facility where this is done at Katale is powered by a hydroelectric plant located on and owned by the estate. The small administrative office in Goma's downtown area facilitates the interface between production and export to the international market. The estate also owns a large depot near the Goma airport that has been rented out to the United Nation peacekeeping forces since 1999.

The creation of the estate and the troubled history of Congo–Zaire intertwine. At independence in 1960, a small plantation located in a place called Katale belonged to a Belgian settler named Van de Vyvere. The other coffee fields that constitute the current estate were owned by other European – mainly Belgian – settlers. According to colonial regulations, plantations could not be larger than 50 hectares, but prices on the international market were high in those years and a family and its workers could earn a decent living with just a few dozen hectares. Today's estate has therefore been pieced together as a mosaic of formerly isolated fields, and it now extends from Katale to Rutshuru. The elders in the area recall that, years ago, elephants roamed the lava plains of Katale and the inhabitants established an ivory market where the production plant now stands.

Post-independence uncertainty and violence pushed the European settlers – including Mr Van de Vyvere – out of the country. A certain Hubert Van Overberghe, however, one of Van de Vyvere's workers, took a chance and offered to buy out his former boss, who accepted. He made similar offers to the other owners, who, frustrated by the poor political context, also acquiesced. Van Overberghe was consequently able to establish and consolidate the estate – and, for twenty years, make it thrive. This ended abruptly in July 1980 when Mr Van Overberghe perished (along with his mechanic) at the controls of his small plane when it crashed into Lake Kivu. Rumours about his attaché case full of money still have currency among the older workers. His widow and children continued to run the estate until 1992, when, fed up with the economic situation of the country and recent pillaging, they decided to sell it to the current owners.

GOOD RELATIONS
MAKE A DIFFERENCE

Economic profitability and the quality of the coffee are fundamental, but maintaining good relations with all the stakeholders in and around the estate is also essential.

We work in an extremely difficult environment, especially since the Rwandan genocide. Nevertheless, we can make ends meet. We're not getting rich but the estate pays a decent salary to us and the staff, and, most importantly, it provides a livelihood to a couple of thousand people. This means a lot to me because social solidarity is so important in this part of the world. War, insecurity and the hassles we've experienced since 1994 have helped us bond. The solidarity shared with neighbours, friends and colleagues in Goma and Rutshuru can be much stronger than in Europe, despite the wide socio-economic divide that exists in the Congo.

Producing and exporting coffee – 'such a noble product' – is a daily challenge to the estate's staff and workers. 'We have to deal with security issues and a volatile international market that we don't control. A great year for Brazilian growers means a less great year for us. But in Kivu, you can accomplish a lot. Our good relations with buyers and transporters help.' The estate has been selling to the same Dutch buyer for over twenty years. 'They know us, appreciate our coffee and like the way we work. They have zero confidence in the country but trust us.' The same applies to relations with the French multinational SDV Bolloré, which handles logistics and transportation. 'Come hell or high water – meaning encounters with men with guns, poor roads or even kidnapping attempts – Bolloré gets our beans to the Kenyan port of Mombasa and then to Europe, Asia and America.'

Emery Malemo Musavuli is a key go-between in these steps. He is the estate's factotum – he serves as the interface between the Goma office and the production team, as well as between the estate and administrative officials. Sometimes his finesse is even needed to keep soldiers around the estate happy: 'A few dollars for beer money usually does the trick.' Fluent in French, Swahili, Kinyarwanda and Lingala, his language abilities help in this environment. His assessment of Isabelle is flattering: 'She is accommodating, hard-working and flexible. And she understands the subtleties of working with us Congolese – and not everyone has that skill.' Emery summarises in Lingala: *'Alingi mobulu te'* ('She doesn't want any problems'). It is noteworthy that Emery and his colleagues address Isabelle as 'Madame', whereas Baudouin is 'the boss'. Asked to be a bit more concrete in his description, Emery gives the following examples:

She is sensitive to African reality, and when there are real problems, she helps. When my first wife died, she paid for the casket, attended the wake and came to the cemetery with the extended family. When armed bandits broke into my house in 2002, I suffered a serious machete wound to my leg. Madame moni-tored and paid for my treatment. The idea of looking for another job has never entered my mind; in fact, my friends are very jealous of my position. Periodic bonuses also help keep us all motivated! Some of my colleagues could earn more by working for interna-tional NGOs or humanitarian agencies but prefer the mood and stability of our company.

'Never underestimate the power of a relationship' is a lesson that Isabelle has learned over her long career in the Congo. Being sensitive to the needs, attitudes and world views of the workers is a golden rule in the estate's management strategy. Indeed, the estate is committed to a social agenda: Isabelle gives advance salary payments in cases of need and hands out cloth, salt and palm oil to the women workers at harvest time. Isabelle and Baudouin have also set up a system of performance bonuses and personal loans. The estate contributes to school fees for workers' children, medical expenses and funeral costs. 'The estate also replaces objects (like mobile phones) stolen by the negative forces so present in our environ-ment.' Also, according to Emery, Isabelle never forgets presents for the New Year and Independence Day.

Emery's opinion is confirmed by Lucas Mulemo, the estate's driver since 2013. 'Madame takes her work to heart; she remembers my wife's name. Management of the vehicles is based on trust.' Lucas, however, is slightly more nuanced in his assessment of Isabelle: 'She never gets angry but we know we have to do exactly as she says.' Isabelle adds that the workers are honest because they realise that sound management is in their own interest. 'Our interests and theirs converge, and the fact that the staff is from the region makes things easier.'

Maintaining good relations with the administrative authorities, notably regarding taxes, is also a concern for the estate. An external chartered accountant works with Mado (the estate's full-time accountant) to make sure that all fiscal responsibilities are respected. 'We are visible so have to be transparent. We comply with our obligations and pay what is required – which explains why we aren't making a fortune. The authorities are lenient with us because the estate commands respect. The fact that we are a member of the Federation of Congolese Enterprises is an additional advantage to help us navigate this potentially complicated administrative landscape.'

The estate is also a member of ASSECCAF (the National Association of Coffee Exporters), which lobbies the government to keep export taxes down. Isabelle and Baudouin have been involved in negotiations to have a fair trade label, but so far in vain. 'Certification is a complicated and expensive undertaking for a small producer like us.' The Congolese National Coffee Board could be a useful partner and provide support, but unlike similar boards in Burundi, Kenya and Rwanda, the Congolese counterpart does not have the means to fulfil its responsibilities.

The estate is respected by local people not only because they have work but also because they are allowed to farm

on its land for their subsistence crops. As people flee insecurity in the highlands they seek refuge in Rutshuru and
Rubare and on the estate's land. This means that there
are more and more people on a shrinking resource base.
'Our excellent relations with the late *mwami* [the local
traditional authority who was also the former Congolese
ambassador to the Netherlands] helped in dealing with
the population influx. He was a real friend. We inciden-
tally helped him acquire books for the public library he
sponsored in Rutshuru.' The estate also worked closely
with the *mwami* and local civil society representatives to
establish a land use management plan.

STRUGGLING WITH A SMILE

The political and security situation could easily have
caused the estate owners to abandon ship if they were
not so deeply rooted in the country. 'Given all the obstacles, it's a miracle that we are still here,' says Isabelle,
who insists on the necessity 'to tread delicately and keep
a smile on your face'. The first major challenge was the
massive arrival of post-genocide refugees. Half a million
of them occupied the estate for two years. 'Luckily, coffee
bushes aren't edible – otherwise they would have been
devoured. We did everything possible to help our people
get through this horrible episode, finding safe havens for
our Tutsi workers, for example.' The estate's health facility
served workers and refugees indiscriminately too. 'We
didn't lose a single worker in the deadly cholera epidemic
of 1994 because we supplied water purification kits.'

To celebrate Bastille Day on 14 July 1994, French soldiers from Operation Turquoise (who were using the Goma airport as a logistical base) were partying on the runway. Baudouin, who was working in a nearby office, had a bird's eye view of the scene. While observing the French soldiers, he noticed thousands of refugees flooding into the city. He called Isabelle, saying: 'Stay put! Don't come into town. Things are going to get crazy.' Indeed, things did get crazy as more than a million refugees crossed over the border in a short period of time. The consequences are still felt in the collective memory of Goma. Isabelle's most vivid recollection of catastrophe relates to water. 'People didn't have clean drinking water and were dying of thirst.'

The human tragedy also resulted in 'the massive and disorderly arrival' of international NGOs and humanitarian organisations. 'The refugees settled in camps, bringing problems and insecurity with them.' Since then, Goma has become a city of expatriates: 'Young humanitarian tourists without vision, driving around in their SUVs. As we get older, they are always in their twenties – faithful to Coco Jambo [a fashionable disco bar] on Friday night and their weekend boat excursions on the lake. When I think about their lifestyles and inefficiency, I don't know whether to laugh or cry.' Isabelle is hardly sympathetic to the humanitarian sector. The epitome of incompetence and narrow-mindedness occurred during a massive cholera epidemic: 80,000 people contracted the disease in the second half of July 1994 – a disease that, from a medical perspective, shouldn't be life-threatening and is relatively easy to cure. 'It is unbelievable that humanitarian agencies extended treatment to refugees but not to the Congolese – justifying the absurdity by the limits of their mandates.' More than thirty years later, people still remember this situation with resentment.

The second major event in the region and therefore for the estate – and, of course, a meaningful page in Congo's/Zaire's history – was the arrival in Goma of Laurent-Désiré Kabila with his famous child soldiers (*kadogos*) at the end of November 1996. A few days later, Kinshasa admitted losing control of Goma (and Bukavu). 'That was a tipping point for us. Uncertainty about our physical security raised a lot of questions, but the fact that the Belgian school shut down didn't leave us much of a choice.' Isabelle consequently returned to Belgium with the three girls – leaving Baudouin to hunker down and carry on with work. Emery added that, when Baudouin had to travel, 'remote control management worked fine thanks to email and the mobile. Even when Madame and the boss weren't here, we were still together.'

In addition to producing and exporting coffee, which is the estate's primary function, it also participates in social development initiatives.

I'm critical but have to admit that not all humanitarians are useless. We've worked with some great NGOs (such as the Dutch branch of Doctors without Borders, Women for Women and Elan) who have produced meaningful results. Women for Women, for example, worked with 400 women from the estate, offering two kinds of assistance. One related to information about health, family planning, women's rights and the management of household money. The second was more technical and taught women how to make soap from local ingredients, manage small restaurants, roast and package coffee, and process local farm products like soy and beans. The estate also worked with a Congolese NGO, Elan – funded by the British Department for International Development – to reinforce workers' capacity to prepare coffee seeds and plants in the framework of a coffee growers' cooperative (Coplacef).

'The estate suffers from the fact that the government doesn't help,' laments Isabelle. 'The difficulties of growing coffee in a highly insecure environment are exacerbated by the disengagement of the state in the coffee sector. If the relevant agencies and ministries helped promote research in new varieties, or disease-resistant varieties, we could easily double our production.' Today, the estate's agronomists reproduce the same seeds and plants that were used before independence. 'These plants simply don't have the strength to produce for a competitive market.' Congolese coffee is also penalised on the international market (specifically by the New York coffee exchange) because of the country's poor reputation and low export production. 'The percentage of Congolese coffee on the world market decreases every year – we currently contribute to around

5 per cent of Congo's total production.' This decrease could create administrative problems down the road if, for example, the state stops granting certificates of origin for export, which is a legal requirement.

The Goma Isabelle first experienced in 1981 is not the same Goma as today. Population growth and spatial expansion are two notable changes. While regretting the absence of a regional development strategy or urban planning policies ('Water, electricity, the roads, waste management – all that is a total fiasco!'), Isabelle prefers to highlight the ways in which people and society have changed.

> Goma has become ever so much more cosmopolitan due to the constant ebb and flow of humanitarian workers and exchanges with neighbouring countries for business and study. Education counts for a lot and parents make whatever sacrifices they can to send their children to schools abroad. Young adults return to Goma speaking English and knowing all kinds of things about computing and high-tech gadgets: I still have my old Nokia – no comparison with the smartphones the Goma youth like to brandish.

She also refers to more troubling tendencies such as targeted killings and kidnappings. 'There are things that I don't want to look into but I know that jealousy, denunciation and retaliation are big problems here. Mafia-type networks control business and ethnicity is a defining factor when it comes to getting a job.' The mushrooming of evangelical churches and the flocks of faithful they attract is another trend that makes her wonder.

The attribute that sums up Isabelle best – and the one that explains her success at managing the Katale Estate – is her heightened sense of caution. Expressions such as 'you have to watch out', 'one never knows', 'be flexible', 'don't lose your temper' and 'show respect' are repeated regularly throughout our discussions. Being attentive to hints and listening to all sides of a story, no matter where people rank on the social ladder (or whether they are Hutu, Tutsi, Nande or Shi – or Congolese or Rwandan), are traits that have become second nature to her.

The future of the Katale Estate depends on the future of the region. The security situation remains uncertain, and although development initiatives are under way, there have been no agreements between local and international stakeholders about what priorities to tackle first. The construction of a hydroelectric power plant in Rutshuru – inaugurated by President Kabila in December 2015 and funded mainly by the super-rich Warren Buffett Foundation along with European Union contributions – in an effort to support conservation of the Virunga National Park, has changed the development complexion of the area. Rehabilitation by the Chinese of the road between Goma and Butembo, which goes through the estate, will also bring change.

Part of the estate will gradually become urbanised, reducing the size of the coffee fields while requiring higher yields. To achieve this, they plan to create new (non-genetically modified) varieties of coffee bushes that could be produced and sold thanks to research partnerships with the French CIRAD agronomy institute and Gembloux. 'Things will certainly change for us and we will probably evolve from our current plantation management towards a nucleus estate model. There are so many factors that we have to consider for our next steps – many of which we cannot control (Will there be another war? Will the Nyiragongo erupt again soon? Will Lake Kivu explode?) – that it is impossible to have a clear picture of where we will be in a few years' time.'

Isabelle's Goma experience has been positive but she remains pragmatic. 'The estate's land is valuable and we will have to sell at some point.' In fact, they have already starting selling off parts of it because the estate's value-added comes more from land for human settlement than from coffee. 'Without work, I won't have any business here. I like and respect our staff but employment and money frame our relations. Once we leave, we won't matter anymore – we'll cease to exist. In any event, we are perceived as white expatriates and nothing can change that.' She says that she may want to return to Goma with her grandchildren just to show them around. Straddling two continents, Isabelle admits with a glimmer of wishful thinking that 'returning to Belgium and sleeping at home without having to constantly worry isn't an unpleasant option'.

CHAPTER 11

VILLAGE BOY
MAKES GOOD

AGAINST ALL ODDS

Papa Martin Mboma is the director of the provincial office of the Federation of Congolese Enterprises (FEC), an organisation that helps formal private business establishments navigate public administrative services. An experienced business professional, he is just as familiar with the latest private investment rules and regulations as with the intricacies of Goma's informal street-based petty trades. Martin was born in 1952 in Kiwandja (on the south side of the Virunga National Park), where his family lived by farming. They grew corn, cassava, vegetables and sugar cane for their own consumption and Arabica coffee for sale in Uganda and Kenya. He attended primary school in his native village and secondary school in the Adventist missionary school in Rwese, where he majored in business administration. In 1973, a year before graduating, his father had a terrible accident and died. He was about to slaughter a wildebeest caught in a trap in his corn field when he was attacked and strangled by a python. The consequences of the tragedy were immediately apparent. 'Who was going to pay my school fees? I was the only boy in the family who had gone to school and would be responsible for taking care of my mother, brothers and sisters.' His fears were slightly exaggerated, however, because thanks to his good marks and conduct, the Adventist fathers waived his fees for his last year.

Based on a strong recommendation from the fathers, he was offered a job teaching accounting at the Kayna Institute upon graduation. At the time, the Zairian economy was still stable and salaries for civil servants and teachers were sufficient to cover basic living expenses and to save. 'I earned enough to take care of my mother and sisters, who stayed with her in Kiwandja. After two years of loyal service, I was promoted to assistant director – a job I held for eight years.' While he was still a teacher, the parents of a seventeen-year-old pupil hired him as a private tutor to help her with homework. The proximity between them led to more than accounting exercises.

Encouraged by my recent promotion, I asked for her hand but was rebuffed, not by her but by her father – even though my family was Nande just like hers. Willibrord, Josephine's father, wasn't opposed to welcoming me into the family as a son-in-law but made it clear that he wanted to marry off his five daughters according to their age: the eldest was to wed first, the last born last. My sweetheart was in third place so Willibrord suggested that if I was in a hurry to start a family, I could marry the eldest sister – Caroline. He was bull-headed and wouldn't budge. I tried to be clever so introduced Caroline and Rachel [the second daughter] to my bachelor friends, hoping for the magic to happen. Patience is a blessing! It took a long four years but the two older sisters found husbands and I was finally allowed to marry my Josephine.

By 1984, Martin and Josephine had two children – which means that he had two families to support. His mother and sisters kept up their farming activities in Kiwandja but were handicapped by not having any men to help with the heavy farming chores. Martin was having a hard time keeping up with his responsibilities. 'My salary was enough to support one family but not two.' He asked an old friend, Rigobert, for advice. Rigobert, who was a lorry driver with TMK (Société de Transports et Messageries au Kivu), informed him that his boss was looking for an accountant for the Goma office. 'TMK was the largest transportation company in the region, covering eastern Congo and East Africa – as far as the Kenyan ports. As I was finding it increasingly difficult to make ends meet in Kayna, I thought that the big city would be a good solution. I travelled to Goma to apply and, thank God, was offered the job.'

CAREER ADVENTURES AND MISADVENTURES

Martin deliberately deceived his colleagues at the Kayna Institute, telling them he needed to stay in Goma for medical care. The Institute continued paying his salary. During his three-month trial period, Josephine remained in Kayna, where she continued her subsistence farming activities. The trial period was a success and he was offered a contract with housing and healthcare benefits. 'It was amazing! I was so happy, especially because I was going to earn five times more than up in Kayna – and the salary was indexed to the foreign exchange market. Modernity was in my reach.' He tended his resignation to the Institute and brought wife and children to Goma, where they lived in the Office neighbourhood. Martin and Josephine left their land and belongings to her family in Kayna for safekeeping.

Martin claims to have led a peaceful life combining work and family pleasures. They had three more children, who studied in Goma's Catholic schools. They moved from Office to Mabanga, near the Notre Dame d'Afrique church. 'By then I was getting regular promotions; we were able to buy a large lot and put up a spacious house. We needed more room, especially as I brought my mother and sisters to Goma to live with us. Altogether we were more than ten.' His mother left their fields and the house with some paternal cousins.

With 1990 came new challenges and the need to make difficult decisions, which nearly upset his good relations with his wife. Through his professional and social networks, Martin was asked to work in the logistics division of the United Nations Industrial Development Organization (UNIDO). 'The dilemma was whether to stick with a secure, well-paying job or take a chance with an international organisation where I would learn and earn more. Josephine plainly opted for the status quo, arguing that a stable job with a permanent contract was better than a risky temporary shift towards the unknown.' But Martin saw things differently. He wanted to get back into a learning environment and broaden his horizons. 'The fact that I never had the opportunity to go to university was a psychological impediment which I wanted to overcome.' Against the wishes of his wife, who had rallied the entire family to her side, Martin wrote his second letter of resignation.

> In addition to salary rewards, UNIDO provided me with a pick-up truck. The kids were delighted to be driven to school and even Josephine had to admit that we had taken a step for the better. After a few months, I had enough money to buy another house lot in the Majengo neighbourhood without having to ask the family to make the slightest sacrifice. The lot – where we still live today – is large enough for a pen to keep animals. There is space for kitchen gardening too. After only six months, the house was nearly completely built.

Martin's stint at UNIDO put him in contact with some ambitious investors while also giving him the opportunity to immerse himself in the United Nations system. 'I perceived a new world opening up to me in terms of professional relationships and the acquisition of useful practical knowledge.' This upbeat attitude was to be demolished suddenly with the September pillaging. 'Everything that UNIDO had done was wiped out overnight. The expatriate staff packed their bags, just hardly saying goodbye, leaving us to deal with our misery. As TMK was also destroyed, Josephine abstained from criticising me.' The income stopped but the expenditures continued. To keep the family afloat, Martin returned to the village to farm while Josephine distilled and sold *kanyanga* (a strong corn-based alcohol). 'Relations with the extended family were not too severely disrupted because everyone was in the same situation.'

Martin was informed that UNIDO was not about to return and that there was no hope of receiving any kind of severance pay. But UNIDO had shared office space with the FEC, and, after months of negotiation, it was decided that the two structures would merge to capitalise on their respective accomplishments. This meant that Martin was eligible for recruitment into the Congolese federation. 'God listened to my prayers for deliverance. Since then – so for over twenty-five years – I've worked for the FEC, gradually climbing the organisational ladder, assuming new responsibilities and travelling to Kinshasa, to other Congolese provinces and even to Europe.'

Firmly engaged in the promotion of business and formal sector employment, Papa Martin proudly waves the banner of his institution. 'The FEC is an association of entrepreneurs that also serves as a chamber of commerce. Our objective is improving the investment environment and attracting local and international investors.' Membership is voluntary and based on an annual fee. Receiving help in the resolution of tax disputes and administrative hassles is the primary motivation for participating. Martin's current challenge is helping potential investors understand eastern Congo. He responds to questions about energy, taxation, investment security, human resources, real estate rental and ownership and the availability of equipment and material. 'I recently spent a few days with a Belgian businessman who is interested in setting up a fruit juice plant.' The double message he tries to get through to the provincial government is that there will be no responsible investment without security and no development without business. Although he plays the role of company man, Martin admits to shortcomings. 'The FEC is dominated by a Mobutu-style mentality, reminiscent of the Association des Entreprises du Zaïre (ANEZA). It exists in part so political authorities can bully the private sector and get money out of it.'

Papa Martin has experienced all kinds of socio-political upheavals and natural disasters in the more than thirty years he has lived in Goma. 'These events have made me pessimistic and a bit fatalistic too, yet paradoxically a bit proud – proud because survival comes naturally to me, as it does to many of the people in the city. I've created my own luck by never letting my guard down.' The family lived through the second wave of pillaging in 1993 with less stress than the first because they had returned to the village and collected their farm tools.

The genocide of 1994 and the refugee crisis had a powerful impact on Martin's spiritual awakening. 'Witnessing the overwhelming suffering of innocent people helped me understand the vanity of the material world.' This coincided with Martin's new job with the FEC and he thought that maybe the situation would stabilise. 'But I was naïve.' In October 1996, the Alliance of Democratic Forces for the Liberation of Congo-Zaire took Goma. 'We truly felt that this was a step towards liberation because the twilight of the Mobutu regime was a stifling period in the Kivus. Immunised by the succession of upheavals, the start of the second Congo war in August 1998 was just one more tragedy to grapple with. The people of Goma have learned to adapt.'

The volcanic eruption of January 2002 was, according to Martin, 'another reminder of how vulnerable we humble mortals are'. Lava covered their lot, destroying the house and everything in it. 'More than anything else, I was sorry to lose old family photos, letters and other papers.' The extended family took them in for the time needed to clear the lot and rebuild the house. Even though they received no outside support or insurance money, they rebuilt in only a few months' time. 'I can't explain how things went so quickly. It's proof that God was looking after my family.'

THE DYNAMISM OF THE INFORMAL ECONOMY

'Goma's expanding population wants to participate in the revolution for modernity, but when you look around, you see all kinds of petty craftsmen and traders whose work modes are incredibly rudimentary.' Papa Martin, the employment sector professional, confirms what any casual observer can easily see: the Goma economy is overwhelmingly informal. Most economic activity in Goma takes place outside the official economy – and this also applies to the entire country. The informal economy includes activities that are unrecorded and, to varying degrees, illegal or illegitimate. They are designed to avoid administrative control and taxation. They include small-scale street vending, trading, cross-border commerce and schemes intended to avoid the payment of taxes on legal production. Smuggling, hustling, pilfering and other unofficial activities also characterise the informal economy of Goma. This way of life provides access to goods and services unavailable in the collapsed official economy, compensating for deficiencies in infrastructure and services, transportation, distribution networks and access to credit. Martin willingly admits that 'in this type of environment, corruption thrives at all levels'.

Twenty-five years of insecurity have exacerbated chronic joblessness in the formal sector. 'Low school attendance and poor-quality instruction have sacrificed a generation of young and not-so-young Congolese. Lots of people here can barely read, write and do simple arithmetic. These handicaps, nevertheless, do not keep them from rolling up their sleeves and getting down to work.' The informal economy has therefore become a kind of refuge for these men and women with few skills but powerful motivation. The strong ones improvise as porters, security guards, masons, *tshukudeurs*, construction workers and waste removers. Others deploy their survival strategies to shine shoes, wash dishes, clean cars, flog cheap goods on the street, drive buses or help as go-betweens in the service sectors.

These jobs are not valued as 'real jobs'; they are something to do while waiting for better opportunities. 'These activities keep people in situations of underdevelopment and poverty. Where are the plans to build a future? They live from hand to mouth without being able to save or invest. Just getting by isn't enough. Moreover, these people are vulnerable and are often taken advantage of by our authorities, who invent taxes and fines to fill their own pockets.' Martins knows of individuals who have had unexpected windfalls (from gambling, an inheritance or a Western Union transfer from abroad) and have started up small businesses. 'With even a small amount of money it is possible to buy a stock of merchandise wholesale and sell it retail.' Psychologically, becoming one's own boss in a small way is important and can lead to ambitious expectations. 'For a big man driving around in an SUV, the guy selling handmade brooms on the street is insignificant. But seeing that big man drive by can lead the broom seller to imagine himself the big boss of all the broom sellers.' Similarly, Martin knows the owner of a large match-producing factory who started out by selling single matchboxes on the street. 'He became rich by earning just a little on lots of volume, not by earning a lot on a few items.'

The employment situation was already bleak for the people of Goma in 1994, but when the refugees arrived it became even worse. 'The refugees were willing to work for practically nothing – a bit of food or a corner of hard lava to sleep on in someone's compound. Then, an equally impressive army of foreign aid agencies and NGOs arrived to relieve their distress.' This second wave of expatriates had an indirect impact on the job market but relatively few people in Goma were eligible or qualified for the better positions. 'Only the menial jobs were open to them. They took them, however, because they thought it more rewarding than returning to their villages to farm.'

Certain jobs that are supposed to be regulated by the appropriate official Congolese legislation are largely neglected by the authorities. 'Contract agreements, sick leave, retirement benefits and arbitration exist more in theory than in practice.' In his professional environment and in his work in the church community, Martin has heard stories from cooks, guards, nannies, shop clerks and others who complain of 'pathetic treatment' from their employers. 'My boss is a real despot who does what he wants with me. He decides how much he will pay me at the end of the month, overloads me with work and treats me like an insect. If I complained, I'd be sacked on the spot – so I just say amen.' Their dilemma is whether to keep their dignity or their job. 'It is humiliating to reconcile the two.'

Women play a significant role in the fend-for-yourself economy. Some notable activities are petty street trade, the preparation and sale of street food, currency exchange, running pharmacies, and all kinds of domestic chores. Many women have climbed the employment ladder by doing a wide range of work. Martin pinpoints their role as accountants, shop assistants and managers, receptionists, bank tellers and public relations experts – and in some cases they can be found in the upper echelons of public administration.

Even though informal economic activities dominate the Goma landscape, formal activities are also important. State public services are the region's largest official provider of employment. This includes most notably the armed services, under the President's jurisdiction (mainly the Armed Forces of the Democratic Republic of Congo or FARDC), and the intelligence services (National Intelligence Agency or ANR). These are followed by the Congolese National Police (PNC) and the Department of Migration (DGM), which are both part of the Ministry of the Interior. These state agents are theoretically paid by central government resources, but Martin repeats what everyone already knows. 'Their salaries – rarely more than $100 a month – do not allow them to live. That is why they use their guns or other symbols of power to squeeze money out of the population.' Provincial ministries, which also employ large numbers of workers, operate along the same lines. 'The state agents with the most enviable positions work in the tax collection agencies or the water and electricity distribution parastatals. The fancy cars and big new villas mushrooming up in Goma belong to them. I guess they have finagled ways to supplement their official salaries.'

The main growth sectors in Goma today are banking and finance, construction, telecommunications and beer. The hotel sector has been flourishing over the past quarter of a century, catering to the expatriate community. Papa Martin sees a huge gap in the deals that can be made in these areas compared with the difficulties most people face to eke out enough money for food. 'Legal and illegal mining also contributes to the fortunes being made in the region and explains why the clients in some fancy restaurants can eat a meal that is worth the equivalent of a few months' salary for a civil servant.' In his opinion, the emergence of an aggressive community of entrepreneurs is linked to these activities.

VICTIMS AND SURVIVORS

Weighing his words carefully, Papa Martin admits that he cannot complain about his lot in life even though he did not have the opportunity to study after finishing secondary school. Thinking that he could help his children get ahead, he encouraged them to pursue university training. 'I thought that degrees would be a shortcut to the success, respectability and well-being that I achieved by taking the long way around.' His son graduated with a law degree but spends his time in a small kiosk where he sells tins of sardines, waffles, bottled water and soap when he is not volunteering in court. 'Luckily, my daughters are all married and are safe and sound.' But, consistent with his anxious nature, he wonders about their future. 'Anything can happen here. The recent history of Goma and the region has been full of surprises. Armageddon will come in a flash. Only the paranoid survive and only the really paranoid can prosper.'

'Despite the dynamism and determination of ordinary people, the government's unenthusiastic efforts to bring about stability and development have failed. There is very little faith in either the provincial authorities or Kinshasa to do much.' Martin is clearly dubious about the capacity of the government and security forces to ward off new rebel movements or invasions. 'On the economic front too, dynamic businessmen and women have turned their backs on the central government because they see better opportunities in East Africa and Asia. Here we know how to plan, but people in Kinshasa do not even understand what the word planning means.' His faith in civil society organisations to channel popular will is hardly more positive. 'Sometimes they get people into the streets to demonstrate but without thinking through the implications of their slogans.' He recalls an incident when people demonstrated in downtown Goma to voice their frustration. They were chanting *'Wafwa wafwa washala washala'* ('There will be victims but there will also be survivors'). From this collective show of determination, Martin reaches his own personal conclusion: 'I'll continue to resist; the main thing is to stay among the living'.

'Suspicious' is probably the epithet that corresponds best to Papa Martin, but he is not averse to taking chances. He does not take unnecessary risks but he does not want to miss opportunities either. In work and in his social relations, he tries to strike the right balance between the two. 'When I lost my father at seventeen, neither I nor anyone else would have imagined that I was destined for a successful career. Instinctively I figured out that good relations with colleagues, friends, family members and even random acquaintances were key to getting ahead. Goma is a school of life that gives out diplomas only after going through a long and arduous apprenticeship.'

Mungu na maombi (God and prayer) are part of Martin's daily life and another factor he sees as having allowed him to be successful. Drivers paint these words on the back of their taxis, and shopkeepers on their kiosk doors. Faith is a decisive part of how Martin sees the world and the way he has defined his identity. 'God', 'Jesus', 'benediction', 'grace', 'miracle' – but also 'the devil', 'apocalypse' and 'damnation' – are some of the spiritual words that punctuate his conversations.

> My faith in the Lord Almighty has got me through some difficult moments. It is thanks to him that I was able to sidestep the traps destiny laid for me and to keep thinking positively about how to deal with the challenges that lay ahead. We've survived lootings, war and the humiliation of an arrogant enemy occupation. We've been attacked but our spirits are unbroken. This

saga of Goma is a lesson to our children who should build their future with tolerance – but without being taken advantage of.

As Martin considers himself blessed from above, he keeps his heart open to the sorrows of others. Deeply committed to his church work in the Notre Dame d'Afrique parish, he does not hesitate to invite people less lucky than himself to the family table or even to pay their school or medical fees. 'In our home, the Lord sits at the centre of the table. My daughters sang in the church choir and my sons were altar boys.' A gigantic pot of beans simmers every first Sunday of the month in his wife's outdoor kitchen. She shares his sense of charity and prepares the beans for the inmates of Goma's Muzenze prison. 'The Lord never abandoned us so how can we neglect these unhappy souls?'

CHAPTER 12

GILDED YOUTH IN SEARCH OF THEIR FUTURE

AN AMAZING CITY

Clarisse Soki sees herself as one of Goma's lucky ones. 'I'm proud to be a *Gomatracienne* and vigorously dispute the reputation that doomsayers have given to my amazing city.' This millennial Congolese woman came to Goma as a baby when her mother decided to leave Katanga, as the floundering copper-producing province lost its economic appeal. Clarisse, who lives in the impressive villa built by her mother in the nice residential Himbi neighbour-hood, graduated from Université Libre des Pays des Grands Lacs (ULPGL) in 2013 with a degree in finance and management. She concedes that her view of Goma is subjective – and certainly not shared by everyone – but that does not seem to ruffle her feathers.

> This city is multifaceted with a full range of social classes. People may not go to the same places or do the same things but they are all part of the landscape. We understand that and appropriate Goma in our own

ways. My Goma of Himbi isn't the same as that of my poor cousins who live in Ndosho. Sometimes our itineraries overlap when we go downtown to take care of administrative business, for example, but there is little overlapping when it comes to schools, shops, health services or recreation. When newcomers arrive here, they want to stay. Neither insecurity nor the volcano can scare away real *Gomatraciens*. When there are problems – and believe me I've experienced them – we come back as soon as the immediate danger has passed. Inspired and determined, just like it says in our national anthem, we rebuild, more beautiful than before.

Clarisse adds that between the nice neighbourhoods of Himbi and Katoyi and the equivalent ones in Kinshasa (Ma Campagne and Mont Fleuri), she prefers her own. She also says that the fleet of new SUVs on Goma's streets is another example of material comfort. 'Their owners are well-to-do people who bought them thanks to their hard work, which is why they like to show off. You can't be a man here if you can't afford to buy your girlfriend at least a RAV4. Honestly, are we supposed to be impressed by the arrogance of the Kinois with their fashion and bossy Lingala?' She wonders what it is like to see Goma for the first time. 'I guess it is hard to figure out how we live in this city because security, employment and commercial conditions are constantly evolving – but that's one of the reasons I love it. If you are competent and strong-willed, you can do well here.'

Gaspard, Clarisse's older brother who studied law, complains that when the central government decides on development funding, Goma is forgotten and systematically gets less than Kinshasa or other more politically important provinces.

> That's why Goma is being built by us *Gomatraciens* who believe in our own capacity. We don't depend on Kinshasa or anyone else. Goma's economic, demographic and spatial expansion has taken place during the darkest periods of the region's history. When we were under the thumb of the capital we were hobbled. Since the rebellions that weakened Kinshasa's control over us, look at how the city has progressed. It seems like Goma thrives on chaos. After a tragic event, the lights come back even brighter.

These dynamics have resulted in the formation of a new class of individuals, which could be likened to an emerging middle class. Gaspard, who clearly shares his sister's perceptions of opportunity and empowerment, suggests that 'even the poor are better off in Goma than elsewhere in Congo. Food is widely available and people eat three meals a day. That is just one reason why people like living here.' The stance of both Clarisse and Gaspard on being part of the lucky few is firm. 'We are not rich but we have quite enough to be comfortable – as long as no new tragedies befall us.' The children owe their status to the talent and hard work of their mother – Elise – who wound up a long career with international organisations as head of human resources with Oxfam UK. Elise built her career on her own without help from anyone – but the road to a comfortable life was not smooth. 'Her ups and downs inculcated in us a sense of wariness and discretion, which explains why we like to keep a low profile. None of us is boastful or arrogant, unlike some of our nouveau riche neighbours who have to flaunt their wealth to prove they exist.'

Clarisse is nevertheless quite content with the Toyota RAV4 her mother bought for her. She uses it to go to class, shop for food (sometimes as far as Sake to buy large quantities of vegetables and *makala*), visit friends, go to her hairdresser and drive to church on Sundays. 'Mama wanted us all to have our driving licence so she wouldn't have to chauffeur us around.' The vehicle also helped Clarisse scour the city when looking for a job. 'I'll need a good job to prepare for my future. Mama will help through her network of international agencies and I'm grateful to her. We are who we are because of her training and discipline.'

THRIVING AMONGST THE RUBBLE

Clarisse Soki was born in Lubumbashi in 1988, the baby of four children. She has an older sister (Audrey) and two brothers (Placide and Gaspard). Her father, Melchior, was an accountant at the Gécamines and her mother worked for the United Nations Industrial Development Organization (UNIDO). Both natives of the Butembo area of North Kivu, they met while studying at the University of Lubumbashi.

Up until their departure from Katanga they were living well, but by the late 1980s the Gécamines was in serious financial and management difficulties and Melchior – who worked in the finance department – saw the writing on the wall. Elise and Melchior decided to return to their native province, but at the last minute Melchior changed his mind and stayed. Elise, however, continued with her plan to reverse migrate. Since that time – Clarisse was four years old – Melchior has been a stranger to his wife and children. Clarisse remembers panicking when she first saw black dust all over the place upon her arrival in Goma. 'Mama just looked at me when I said I wanted to return to Lubumbashi and reunite with Papa. My brothers and sisters were not as taken aback as I was because they were curious about our new surroundings. But Mama was determined to take the bull by the horns and make a go of it even without any help from Papa.'

A distant cousin of Melchior put them up for a few weeks in Mabanga, which was then one of the poorest areas of Goma. 'The houses were built of wooden planks and the streets covered in rubble. I remember the place as being dirty and horrible. We didn't make friends with our neighbours, who we found to be very ill-behaved. There wasn't even a decent toilet.' For the sake of her children, Elise found another place to live. 'Mama was afraid that we would drown in the lake because we used to go and play down there while filling our water jugs. Of course, there was no running water in Papa's cousin's house.' They moved to the Virunga neighbourhood, where Elise rented a house. 'Even though it was also made of planks, it was neatly arranged, clean and even had electricity.' Their school was nearby so they would invite their classmates to play after class. 'We were so proud to have kids over to show off our electric train and the other toys we brought with us from Lubumbashi. We made friends and got good marks at school – it was a youthful period of *joie de vivre*.'

Elise, in the meantime, was unemployed. Confident that her experience at UNIDO would open doors for her, she applied to all the United Nations agencies, other international organisations and NGOs. 'All of this was in vain – I didn't even get an interview.' To make ends meet, she sold used clothing on credit that a university friend sent her from Kinshasa.

> I didn't earn much but it was enough to pay the rent, buy food and pay school fees. It wasn't hard work and it wasn't difficult to find customers – many of whom were parents from the Catholic school my kids attended. I just had to be careful to keep up the inventory and not sell to people who wouldn't respect their debts. Goma's strategic location facilitated trade with East Africa too. All in all, I had the feeling that I was going to be able to put roots down in Goma and make a decent living.

Her business expanded and she travelled to Kampala, Nairobi, Mombasa and Dar es Salaam to purchase stocks of used clothing and small household consumer goods. Her little sister came down from their home village of

Muhangi (50 kilometres north-west of Butembo) to take care of the children during these buying expeditions. 'I was satisfied with the way things were going for myself and the way the kids were progressing at school. My instinct that Goma would be a place of opportunity was slowly being confirmed. As I was far from desperate, I continued applying for jobs but only selectively.'

In April 1993, Elise applied for and was offered a job as assistant to the administrative and financial director of the Dutch branch of Doctors without Borders. The computer skills she had acquired with UNIDO in Lubumbashi were an advantage in her application. 'As my used clothing business was going well, I hesitated in accepting the position. But they wanted me and made an offer I couldn't refuse: a generous salary with a permanent contract, a housing allowance, a health benefit package and a contribution to school fees.' Elise therefore found herself back in the fold of Congo's international aid environment. Not only was her little sister useful in watching over the children, she also took over the small boutique where Elise sold her imported household goods and used clothes at the Virunga market. The year Elise started with Doctors without Borders was an important transition year for Goma and the region. She recalls seeing the city develop in front of her eyes.

There was plenty of money in the hands of business people, military officers, high-ranking civil servants and mineral traders. My own situation wasn't bad either. My kids went to the best schools and I could see myself catching up with the rich entrepreneurs who saw themselves as something special. We had moved into a new house where we could welcome friends without the least feeling of inferiority. Nothing seemed to prevent me from thinking about sending my children to study in Kampala, Nairobi – and, why not, even America. Within a year, however, the big catastrophe hit.

Clarisse, who was six at the time, witnessed the arrival of the refugees and the ensuing cholera epidemic. 'I remember seeing people dropping dead and lorries carrying the corpses to common graves that were dug with dynamite. Schools shut down but that didn't prevent Gaspard from contracting cholera. Some of our classmates died, but thanks to Mama's medical contacts at work he was saved. That's what motivated my big sister Audrey to study pharmacology at university.'

'This was the time when the big rush of humanitarian agencies arrived,' recalls Elise. 'Lots of people in my circle of acquaintances were recruited and were offered salaries of up to $2,000 a month – a lot of money in Goma at the time. This money contributed to the development of the city and to the wild circulation of dollars. Lots of families – like my own – were to profit from the tragedy.'

CONFLICT AND DISASTER

Doctors without Borders evacuated the family to Bujumbura, along with its expatriate staff, when the Alliance of Democratic Forces for the Liberation of Congo-Zaire

(AFDL) took Goma in February 1996. The evacuation was short-lived and they returned to Goma after a week. Eight years old, Clarisse remembers how people expressed the sentiment of being liberated from an oppressive dictatorship. 'The AFDL soldiers had a friendly reputation – unlike Mobutu's men who were hated for the way they terrorised people.'

Elise quit Doctors without Borders in June 1999 because Oxfam UK offered her a better job with more rewards. They left the apartment she had been renting downtown and moved to Katindo – but the children did not have to change schools. She drove them herself in the first car she had bought (a Mazda 626). The $1,500 she received every month as a housing allowance was enough to cover rent and to save for the purchase of the lot where she built her villa. 'Financially I was doing well, and as I travelled regularly, my salary was supplemented with generous per diem allowances. Thanks to my sister's help, my side business was profitable too. With all this I could take care of all the kids' needs while also helping out the extended family – by taking in relatives to live with us, for example.'

While Elise was getting used to her new job and status, another tragedy befell Goma: the Congolese Rally for Democracy (RCD) invaded the city in August 1998, marking the beginning of the second Congo war. 'It was an absolute nightmare for us because we were separated with no way of communicating.' Clarisse had just entered secondary school and Audrey was about to graduate. The invasion took place during the day when Elise was at work and the children at school. Audrey, Placide, Gaspard and Clarisse made it home but their mother was stranded at work in another part of town. As there had been rumours that an invasion was looming, Elise had given careful instructions about what to do: 'Stay home and wait for me.' Despite these instructions, they were persuaded by well-intentioned (but meddlesome) neighbours to flee with them towards Sake – outside the city. Mobile phones were not common then so they could not let their mother know where they were.

It was a stressful walk to Sake, which they reached safely along with groups of other people fleeing. They were offered shelter in a Protestant church where they stayed for a week. 'By then, word had got around that Goma was safe and people were adapting to the new RCD administration, so we headed home. We were reunited with our mother who was beside herself with grief. "Praise the Lord" was the first thing she said when she saw us.' Much of Elise's merchandise at the Virunga market had been looted but her savings were sufficient to start over again. 'We survived this episode thanks to our prayers.' As the population gradually became acclimated to the new regime, yet another disaster struck on 17 January 2002 – and this time Elise lost just about everything she owned.

We knew that Nyiragongo was rumbling. Tremors had been felt in Gisenyi and the authorities had sounded the alarm. But people still went about their business not imagining that the lava would reach the city. But that is exactly what happened. Oxfam evacuated us to Kigali by road where we stayed for ten days. Upon our return, we discovered the magnitude of the damage. Lava had destroyed my boutique at the market and our rental house in Katindo. Between losing my merchandise and having to replace all kinds of things from clothing to furniture, the construction of the house in Himbi was put on hold for a couple of years.

The house Elise was eventually to build – and move into during the summer holidays of 2009 – is an impressive brick structure on a spacious lot (60 metres by 50) in a good location, again confirming Goma's reputation as a city of opportunity. It has fourteen rooms, four full bathrooms, verandas in the front and back, an inside kitchen with an electric stove and an outside one to cook with *makala*. The electricity and plumbing were top quality at the time of installation, even though there is no running water in the neighbourhood and there are frequent electricity black-outs. A four-room house made of planks sits in a corner of the lot for visitors or renters. The rest of the lot is covered in green: there are ornamental flowers and bushes, fruit trees, a lawn and a kitchen garden where the servant girl grows beans, sweet potatoes, cassava and corn. There is no garage but there is enough additional space for at least six vehicles. This is all surrounded by a high lava-stone wall topped with razor wire to keep intruders out.

GREAT EXPECTATIONS

The series of catastrophes has affected Clarisse and others from her social class more psychologically than practically. 'Our parents are there to take care of us. We can go to university, spend money and enjoy life. Soon enough we will have to do the same thing for our children once we have jobs and our own families.' Before graduating, Clarisse would spend time with friends after class, either at their homes or in internet cafés where they would work on their assignments. Some afternoons they would drive to the centre and window shop or buy things. Respectful of the strict education she received, Clarisse appears judgemental of the 'irresponsible drinking and late-night activities' of some of her acquaintances. 'Goma is dangerous after dark. My friends organise parties at the weekends in the afternoon so we can be home by 7 pm.' Elise was less successful in keeping her sons on the same track. Placide, whose nickname in the family is 'Party Boy', was a regular in Goma's bars and nightclubs. 'But after Mama locked the gate and kept them outside a couple of times, they got the message and complied with her rules.'

Audrey finished her degree in pharmacology in 2010 and shortly afterwards married a doctor whom she met at university in Nairobi, where they both studied. Elise was happy with the union because she knew the boy's family from the village in the north. Audrey works for Merlin, an international medical NGO, and Freddy, her husband, works for another NGO that offers medical services to people in areas held by rebels. He spends most of his time in the field, able to return to Goma and his wife when on short-term leave. They have their own home, which was designed by Placide.

Placide recently moved back to Goma from Kinshasa, where he studied architecture. To keep up with his life-style, Elise bought a minivan for him which he used as a taxi. According to his little sister, 'His reputation as "Party Boy" was confirmed in Kinshasa but that didn't stop him from getting his degree, and we know he has talent because he has voluntarily helped people in our circle of friends design their homes while waiting to get a paid position.'

Gaspard studied law at the same university as Clarisse and graduated in 2012. When he is not in the field on short-term assignments for NGOs promoting human rights, he lives in the family villa. He plans to become a lawyer but hasn't found the energy or opportunity to prepare for the bar exam. 'I don't know what's the matter with that boy,' wonders Elise. 'Perhaps I made it too easy for him. I think the material comforts I've provided have made him soft.'

When Clarisse graduated, she proved to have real gumption in her search for work – hand delivering letters, making phone calls, getting advice about how to write her résumé, looking at bulletin boards and talking to as many people as possible. In the meantime, she took English classes. Her efforts paid off and within a year she was hired by an international NGO. Her mother, who has different kinds of worries for each child, is concerned about Clarisse's private life. 'The girl is smart and has plenty of charm but I haven't seen any boyfriends coming around. I have no inkling about her affairs of the heart and she doesn't volunteer any information. I'm probably an over-anxious mother and just hope things will work out for her.'

Elise also admits that she is very proud of her offspring and happy about the way she has been able to help them grow up to be responsible adults. This feeling has been reinforced over the past year because her health has seriously declined. 'My high blood pressure, complicated by hyperglycaemia, almost sent me to the grave. Fortunately, I had the money to go to India for treatment, accompanied by Audrey.' Still fragile and nearly blind, she had to end the career that allowed her to take charge of her destiny.

Growing up in Goma during these troubled decades has not been easy for Clarisse and her siblings, even though they readily admit how much luckier they are than most. Clarisse's sense of well-being goes beyond 'the vanity of material things'. Friends and family, her studies, travel and work are the reasons why she has confidence in herself. 'A new pair of jeans and a night on the town are not going to make me happy, unlike lots of my acquaintances who live by short-term expedients. I don't like seeing people waste their potential.' An expression used in Goma to describe extravagant and ostentatious behaviour is 'drink water with a fork'. Clarisse resolutely keeps her distance from that kind of behaviour and proudly summarises the image she tries to create for herself: 'I'm ambitious, enterprising and determined. I'm thirsty for independence and want to associate with the young adults of Goma who share my drive to get ahead.'

AFTERWORD

Between the time when I first had the idea to write about Goma's social dynamics and the publication of this version in English, some things have stayed the same in DRC and others have evolved. The political situation has deteriorated because of President Joseph Kabila's stubborn grip on power: the elections that were supposed to have been held in December 2016 have been postponed until an uncertain future date. Goma's citizens took to the streets in protest, some paying for resistance with their lives. Congo's main export commodities have lost value on global markets, reducing revenues and fiscal earnings, shrinking an already inadequate national budget. The Congolese franc has lost 40 per cent of its value so far this year and inflation is expected to exceed 30 per cent by the end of 2017. Civil servants have gone on strike, frustrated by the fact that their salaries remain unchanged. One colleague from Kinshasa confided to me: 'With a hundred dollars, I could buy enough rice and charcoal for the month; but now, those hundred dollars don't last more than two weeks.' Political opposition is fragmented, a situation exacerbated by the death of veteran opposition leader Étienne Tshisekedi. Violence in the formerly peaceful Kasai region has caused over a million people to flee their villages: Kamwina Nsapu rebel militia decapitated forty-two police officers and murdered two United Nations experts. Ongoing insecurity reigns in the Kivus. These are the kinds of issues commonly associated with Congo beyond its borders as reported by the media and studied by researchers.

The complexion of Goma is evolving relentlessly too. Roads in the city centre are being paved, the pace of peri-urban house construction continues, and international partners are helping with water distribution efforts. President Kabila opened a 13.6 megawatt hydroelectric power station at Matebe. Initiated by the Congolese Institute for Nature Conservation and funded by the Howard Buffett Foundation, it is expected to decrease Goma's reliance on charcoal from the Virunga Park. Liboko the charcoal man is still involved in the trade, which, nevertheless, has not yet shown signs of diminishing.

Clarisse Soki has found work in an international NGO but lost her mother: Mama Elise, who offered us assistance and inspiration, passed away before seeing this book in print. Asumani the *motard* also passed away, and Cerezo the *tshukudeur*, worn out from a hard life, is housebound. Eric is still active in his parish and earning a living with his Canadian drilling company. Mathilde has regained her vitality and is combining various business deals while helping take care of new grandchildren. Celestin and Mituga – the stonecutters who have 'stopped dreaming' – are still carrying on with their work and friendship. Papy is going strong with The Warrior Security and Mama

Betty's bean business is keeping her and Georges busy. Papa Martin's ongoing commitment to the FEC mission gives testimony to the relative stability of Congolese civil servants in a harsh investment environment – but an environment that has not discouraged Isabelle and Baudouin Michel enough for them to sell the coffee estate.

In December 2016, I had the opportunity to present the French version of this book in Goma. When I hand delivered a copy to Dr Chantal Sasolele at her home, she first smiled, then shed tears of joy. 'When my little girls are older and read my story as related in this book, they'll ask me "Is all this really true about you and Papa, about the refugees, about how you lived then …?"' She also described her daughters' future vision about trade and transport, housing and infrastructure and human relations – wondering out loud, 'What will Goma be like when my daughters are my age?' These stories – those of Chantal and the others – offer a glimpse of how life goes on in Goma – this city that is not only a place of endless suffering but also one of opportunity, friendship, romance and hopes for a better tomorrow.

Theodore Trefon
Washington DC
August 2017

NOTES

INTRODUCTION

1 Armin Rosen (2013) 'A day in the DRC', *The Atlantic*, 21 May, http://www.theatlantic.com/international/archive/2013/05/a-day-in-the-drc/276038/.

2 Séverine Autesserre (2010) *The trouble with the Congo: local violence and the failure of international peacebuilding*, New York: Cambridge University Press.

3 Silke Oldenburg (2010) 'Under familiar fire: making decisions during the "Kivu crisis" 2008 in Goma, DR Congo', *Africa Spectrum*, 45 (2): 61–80.

4 Some of the more notable work that focuses specifically on Goma is that by Sarah Bailey (2015) 'Review of Norwegian Refugee Council urban assistance in Goma, DRC', Oslo: Norwegian Refugee Council; Karen Büscher and Mathys Gillian (2013) 'Navigating the urban "in-between space": local livelihood and identity strategies in exploiting the Goma/Giseyi border' in Benedikt Korf and Tim Raeymaekers (eds) *Violence on the margins: states, conflict and borderlands*, New York: Palgrave Macmillan; Martin Doevenspeck (2011) 'Constructing the border from below: narratives from the Congolese–Rwandan state boundary', *Political Geography*, 30 (3): 129–42; Silke Oldenburg (2015) 'The politics of love and intimacy in Goma, Eastern DR Congo: perspectives on the market of intervention as contact zone', *Journal of Intervention and Statebuilding*, 9 (3): 1–18; Silke Oldenburg (2010) 'Under familiar fire: making decisions during the "Kivu crisis" 2008 in Goma, DR Congo', *Africa Spectrum*, 45 (2): 61–80; Anna Verhoeve (2004) 'Conflict and the urban space: the socio-economic impact of conflict on the city of Goma' in Koen Vlassenroot and Tim Raeymaekers (eds) *Conflict*

and social transformation in eastern DR Congo, Ghent: Conflict Research Group; Koen Vlassenroot and Karen Büscher (2009) 'The city as frontier: urban development and identity processes in Goma', Working Paper 61, London: London School of Economics.

5 Karen Büscher (2011) 'Violent conflict, state weakening and processes of urban transformation in the eastern Congolese periphery. The case of Goma', unpublished PhD thesis, University of Ghent.

6 The following list is not exhaustive but a few of the more noteworthy works include those by Séverine Autesserre (2014) *Peaceland: conflict resolution and the everyday politics of international intervention*, New York: Cambridge University Press; Séverine Autesserre (2010) *The trouble with the Congo: local violence and the failure of international peacebuilding*, New York: Cambridge University Press; Gauthier de Villers (2009) *République démocratique du Congo. De la guerre aux élections: L'ascension de Joseph Kabila et la Troisième République (janvier 2001 – août 2008)*, Tervuren/Paris: Institut africain-CEDAF/L'Harmattan; Pierre Englebert and Denis Tull (eds) (2013) 'République démocratique du Congo: terrains disputés', *Politique Africaine*, 129; René Lemarchand (2009) *The dynamics of violence in central Africa*, Philadelphia: University of Pennsylvania Press; Gérard Prunier (2009) *From genocide to continental war: the 'Congolese' conflict and crisis of contemporary Africa*, London: Hurst; Filip Reyntjens (2009) *The great African war: Congo and regional geopolitics, 1996–2006*, Cambridge: Cambridge University Press; Jason K. Stearns (2011) *Dancing in the glory of monsters: the collapse of the Congo and the great war of Africa*, New York: PublicAffairs; Denis Tull (2005) *The reconfiguration of political order in Africa: a case study of North Kivu (DR Congo)*, Hamburg: African Studies Institute; Thomas Turner (2007) *The Congo wars: conflict, myth & reality*, London and New York: Zed Books; and Jean-Claude Willame (2010) *La guerre du Kivu: vues de la salle climatisée et de la véranda*, Brussels: GRIP.

7 Patrick Vinck, Phuong Pham, Suliman Baldo and Rachel Shigekane (2008) 'A population-based survey on attitudes about peace,

justice, and social reconstruction in eastern Democratic Republic of Congo', Berkeley and New Orleans: Berkeley-Tulane Initiative on Vulnerable Populations.

8 Georges Berghezan and Xavier Zeebroek (eds) (2011) *Small arms in eastern Congo: a survey on the perception on insecurity*, Brussels: GRIP.

9 Justine Brabant with Kivu fighters (2016) *Qu'on nous laisse combattre, et la guerre finira*, Paris: La Découverte; Ben Rawlence (2012) *Radio Congo: signals of hope from Africa's deadliest war*, London: Oneworld.

10 Mary Jo Maynes, Jennifer L. Pierce and Barbara Laslett (2008) *Telling stories: the use of personal narratives in the social sciences and history*, Ithaca, NY: Cornell University Press.

11 Rosario Giordano (2008) *Belges et Italiens du Congo-Kinshasa: récits de vie avant et après l'Indépendance*, Paris: L'Harmattan.

CHAPTER 3

1 In early 2017, the price of a bag of *makala* in Goma was $35.